SKILLS FOR SURVIVAL

Esther Dickey

HOW
FAMILIES CAN PREPARE

INTERNATIONAL STANDARD BOOK NUMBER
0-88290-093-5

LIBRARY OF CONGRESS CATALOG CARD NUMBER
78-52124

Second Printing, May, 1980

Printed in the
United States of America
by
Horizon Publishers
& Distributors
P.O. Box 490
50 South 500 West
Bountiful, Utah 84010

Preface

Personal peace and self-confidence grows with each new level of family preparedness we achieve. Through careful preparation we can free ourselves from concern over the impact of world situations or personal problems such as economic collapse, drought, famine, energy crisis, illness, reduced standard of living, unemployment, war, death, or natural disasters.

In this choice land we have the greatest asset in the world in preparing for the future. We have the freedom to think, create and develop new ideas to solve the problems of an uncertain future.

There is increasing evidence today of the need to prepare for a changed way of life. Most of the last two generations in this country have never known "want." It isn't easy to prepare until we are convinced of the need or benefits to us personally.

Sure, to be prepared for possible emergencies we need foodstuffs basic to the preservation of life. We need wheat, powdered milk, honey or sugar, salt, maybe some peanut butter or raw peanuts, tomato juice, food supplements, seeds to plant, some beans, a little rice, corn and perhaps other grains, a little meat, dehydrated foods, candles, work clothes, and soap and water. We can go out tomorrow and buy all these things, if we have the money; and if we don't, maybe we could sell something, or borrow the money.

However, at this point, I'm as concerned about *emotional* preparedness as I am about temporal preparedness. How we think about the future will have a great deal to do with how we act and feel physically. "As a man thinketh, so is he" is not a new concept.

In order to cope with the future, and not be depressed, we will need all the latest tools of mind control we can get. These training techniques have come forth at a time when the world needs them most, and are being taught across the nation to businesses, colleges, industries, athletic teams, and in prisons.

I feel that if disasters and hard times come, the ones that survive will be the "elite command"—and there will be a separation of wheat and tares! Calm assurance comes from being ready to accept what comes. I have made a bold definite commitment that I, Esther Dickey, am going to be ready, if necessary, to give birth to a new way of life in dignity and peace. How? Besides the *things* I have stored, I have a bright mental picture of living as my grandparents did:

—Getting water from other sources than from my five domestic water faucets.
—Wearing darker clothes with white collars and accessories to keep clean easier.
—Walking, walking, walking—to church, school, music lessons, etc. (in walking shoes, not high heels or sandles).
—Raising a little meat—rabbits, chickens, a goat or calf.
—Planting food crops, harvesting them, and preserving the surplus.
—Gathering greens from the fields and ditchbanks in the spring.
—Keeping warm in the winter and cool in the summer the way old-timers did—in the shade of a big tree or around the stove.
—Burying our dead.
—Waging a war against rats and mice.
—Staying close to home.

But we need to envision the possibility of serious events which can result if man allows civilization to abandon its reason and balance:

—Nuclear fallout, explosions, fires, burns, hair falling out, nausea, weakness for some.
—Famine in many parts of the world.
—More people banding together for safety—some gravitating to urban areas; others leaving for a place of refuge they have prepared.
—Widespread death and destruction—of people, animals, and plants.
—Violence such as our ancestors could never conceive.
—Degradation of the human race.

With these possibilities growing more real each year, it is becoming increasingly obvious that we must truly be a prepared people.

Someone said we have grasped the mysteries of the atom and rejected the Sermon on the Mount. Ours is a world of nuclear giants and ethical infants. We know more about war than about peace. We know more about killing than we do about freedom—personal freedom as well as political.

I'm always thankful for the support of my husband, family and friends. With them I feel confident I can have comfort, peace, beauty, dignity and order before, during and after these experiences if they occur. Learning is not without anxiety, fears and efforts. We need to help each other learn. I want to put my arms around many people in thankfulness for their great contribution to the cause of family preparedness.

Like a duck, I seem to be paddling furiously under water in order to be calm and undisturbed on the surface when my life style may change—not by choice. I've tried to "tell it like it is." Hopefully my readers can vicariously get the vision of what is ahead in some areas. With additional research and preparation, none of us need fear the future. We can be a prepared people.

While this book covers emergencies, gardening, and foods, it is by no means intended to be an exhaustive study in these areas—merely an effort to "whet the appetite" of the reader and stimulate the desire to "be prepared."

The Author

Acknowledgements

My greatest thanks goes to my husband, Russell, for his prayers, patience and encouragement during the writing of this book. He and other family members have had to put up with me as I constantly feel impelled to pull away from a normal comfortable existence and experience the unknown. For example, my husband and I recently lived in an underground home for five days. Other years, we have lived on four foods; or planted, weeded and harvested 101 different kinds of plants—eating strange things. We turned off the utilities for ten days and lived without heat, light and water from customary sources. Gratitude goes to my family for their support at these times especially.

Thanks also to my brothers, sisters, in-laws, parents, children and friends for their love and understanding and many hours of help in preparing the manuscript.

I am indebted to people throughout much of the world for teaching me ways to adjust to what I would consider intolerable situations. Travels, books, experiences shared by members of audiences, have all influenced me and contributed to the writing of this book.

I often petitioned my Father in Heaven for discernment as to what information would be most needed in the future. I give thanks for the help I received.

Table of Contents

PART I
A CHANGED WAY OF LIFE

TABLES

DRAWINGS AND ILLUSTRATIONS

Part I

A Changed Way of Life

Chapter 1

Family Independence

THERE IS NO QUESTION about the fact that we live in a dependent, complex society. We depend on a multitude of specialists to provide us with both the necessities and the comforts of life.

Family Business Directory

If we were independent of the world, a family business directory would look something like this:

—Automotive and repair shop
—Beauty and barber shop
—Carpenter, plumbing and electrical services
—Music, hobby, recreation, church center and supplies
—Clothing, sewing, yardage and variety story
—Emergency hospital, pharmacy and drugstore
—Power and fuel company
—Hardware store, sporting goods and gun shop
—Hotel and restaurant supplies
—Laundry and dry cleaning
—Miller, bakery, cannery
—Supermarket
—Office supplies and machines
—Seed and garden supply
—Shoe making and repair shop

If all these things went on under your roof, think of:

—The skills and trades involved,
—The tools, equipment and supplies you would need,

—The financial planning needed to acquire them,
—The necessary inventory of foods and proper storage,
—The physical, social, emotional and spiritual strength needed to meet these challenges and stresses with confidence and stability.

We must remember to "not run faster nor labor more than we have strength." It is encouraging to contemplate more and more exchanges of professional services, common labor and goods in a manner similar to the old barter system.

Realizing our inadequacies in these areas could make us feel discouraged about achieving family independence. But there are some bright lights: think of the skills we can learn from college classes and trade schools, from paperback how-to-do-it books and correspondence courses.

Many people become very discouraged when they approach some kind of mechanical skills that they have never attempted before such as plumbing, auto repair and electrical work. In many cases if a person will slow down long enough to study carefully how the item is made, he can figure out how it should be functioning and can solve the problem. There seems to be a growing activity among many hardware stores to sell more and more equipment, tools and supplies for "do-it-yourselfers."

The purpose and intent of this section is to increase the family's independence generally, and decrease the family's dependence on society.

Check List

A list one family is using for a higher level of preparedness is to:

—Build up health and physical condition; exercise regularly.
—Get needed surgery and dental work done.
—Stock durable fabrics and shoes.
—Collect books on survival, gardening, first aid, carpentry, etc.
—Save necessary medicines and food supplements.
—Store fuel for cooking and warmth.
—Install an underground gasoline storage tank, properly vented.
—Have a family organization that operates independently of the outside world.
—Take a trial run. Live for a time on a storage program.

What is the connection between storage areas (explained in the following section) and family independence? For me, I need to find things quickly, have an orderly home, and not waste food and supplies. Efficiency on the home front gives me more time to exercise, garden, learn new things, sort, store, organize and help others.

Order and Convenience of Home Storage Areas

Discard, Rearrange

Few homes have ideal storage space for a year's supply of food and necessities. When our existing space is filled, the only solution seems to be adding on a room or building more shelves or closets. This may or may not be necessary. Often we can sort, discard and rearrange things. How important will some of the stored items be in five or ten years, compared to food?

The quickest way to find a place for something is to find the logical place you think that item should be stored. Remove whatever is in the way. Fill the storage space with your top priority items first, and with great speed dispose of the rest—or find a new home for it. (If you are sentimental about too many "keepsakes," invite a friend you trust to assist you in the painful decisions.) My current motto when housecleaning is "store the best, leave the rest." If you can't part with items you think someone might need someday, box them up, label them, and get them out of sight.

Advantage of Order — I appreciated order more than ever during a recent 10-day trial period in our home of going without electricity,

Store food and supplies in an orderly fashion.

running water or central heating. I could find things even in the dark. I didn't stumble over things in the storage areas when I forgot to take a flashlight. Besides, orderly surroundings kept up my morale.

Having things in order helps in taking inventory. For example, we need to know how much brown rice, oils and nuts we have on hand so we can use them before they go rancid; or we may want to share or exchange with someone. If we found we were out of certain items such as matches, soap and toilet tissue, we would have a problem if we couldn't buy any more.

Convenience — The old adage is to "store what you use and use what you store." If your wheat is in a 50-gallon barrel at the

Store food and supplies
in easily accessible containers.

back of the garage, under another 50-gallon barrel, with other things in front of it, you're not likely to use it. If you had it in easily accessible five-gallon containers, and placed some wheat in a glass jar on a kitchen shelf where you could see it, chances are you would pour out a cup now and again for sprouting or cooking.

Labeling — If we buy in bulk, we have an added responsibility of repackaging, labeling and "storekeeping." "Shopping" at home should be as pleasant as at the supermarket. There would be many dissatisfied customers if business places were dark, dirty and unsightly, if labels were illegible or upside down, or if there were no labels at all. I have solved the problem of good labeling in three ways:

—Masking tape and a waterproof pencil. (Print before cutting tape off the roll.)
—"Stick-on" raised labels made with an embossing machine.

—Self-sticking file folder labels (use thumb tacks on wood shelves if the labels don't stick).

Storage Areas in Unconventional Places

I discovered a new storage area in my home behind an Oriental screen against a north wall. Here I keep eight suitcases packed and labeled together with our sleeping bags. Collecting things from every part of the house, making decisions and packing, was a week's work. The cases are my flight kits; ready to take out of the house at a moment's notice for camping trips or emergency use. They contain the following supplies:

—Food for two weeks and necessary equipment and supplies to prepare and serve it.
—Emergency clothes for hot and cold weather and waterproof gear.
—Expanded first aid and home nursing supplies.
—Drapes and covering for shelter walls.
—Miscellaneous tools and equipment to build and make a shelter more like home.

Having organized supplies in one place has instilled within me a feeling of calm assurance that I can cope with whatever comes.

In touring through many homes and observing their food and supply storage areas, I feel the following suggestions would be helpful:

Use high and low places like a shelf near the ceiling, under stairways (check local fire laws for this), under the house on sheets of plastic, under the bed or baby's crib.

Reduce the size of the room a little with a wood panel or drape on a rod concealing storage against a wall.

Build narrow shelves against a wall with a mural in front.

Take advantage of attic storage. If you have an attic, you're lucky. If you need the storage space and there is no other access, put in a disappearing stairway. Attic storage is for items not affected by extreme temperatures, such as clothing, bedding, paper goods and objects of metal, wood, glass, plastic and leather. Properly insulated attics can be used for food storage. In one family's hot attic, there was a storage space about 64 cubic feet boarded off and insulated with styrofoam sheets. The space was kept cool by a wooden shaft about six inches square going up through the hall ceiling from under the house.

Food on the move: In small apartments, move food from the coldest outside wall in the winter to an inside wall or closet in the summer. If you are not home, cover the window with a cardboard lined with aluminum foil to keep out the heat.

Storage away from home: Buy a metal shed or rent space in a warehouse, or your parents may have room. The Chinese bury grain in the ground in slick surface earthenware pots.

Tool storage: Family members need to know where to find home repair tools and how to use them. The men folks aren't always at home to fix leaks, broken windows, and plugged plumbing in times of trouble—or in times of peace either.

Storage containers as functional furniture:

1. In a crowded apartment one girl had a table-height convenient working space. It was a mattress in the bedroom over the permanent food storage. (Her husband, however, wasn't too happy about climbing "up" to bed.)
2. Wood veneer boxes over five gallon cans of wheat could be used as end tables.
3. Put a skirt around a card table with storage underneath.
4. Bean bag chairs could be filled with beans or wheat instead of tiny plastic pellets.
5. Uniform containers on a closet floor or against a wall could be covered and used for a seat.

An effective do-it-yourself life style and storage program requires planning and organization, but it can be a very creative experience. Let your imagination take wings! Enjoy the assurance of knowing you're less and less dependent on society.

Chapter 2

Home-Produced Products

MEAT, MILK AND HONEY may not always be available in stores and can be produced at home, as can other products.

Meat, Milk and Honey

Raising rabbits is an inexpensive way to produce meat for the family. For the past ten years a family in California has enjoyed their own rabbit meat. Three reasons for raising rabbits instead of chickens are:

—There is twice as much meat on a rabbit.
—The meat tastes about like chicken except it is a little firmer.
—Rabbits are quieter than chickens, not as smelly, and much easier to dress.

A family in Germany fed their rabbits entirely on what they raised, winter and summer: grass and alfalfa and root crops. The root crops were stored in a pit for winter feeding. Cooked potatoes were also fed to the rabbits in the winter, as well as table scraps all year. In this country most rabbits eat prepared pellets, or wheat, oats, grain sorghum, rye or barley, along with their greens.

Two does and a buck produce 40 to 50 rabbits a year, about 180 pounds of meat. If you have a space 4 x 10 feet, you can raise rabbits. They take very little care if you have self-cleaning hutches and automatic watering and feeding devices. They can stand a lot of cold weather, but they need protection from heat.

Recently, my husband dressed eight rabbits. We now have 16 pounds of meat in the deep freeze. It was unbelievable to see the rabbits grow white and fluffy and almost as big as their mother in just two months. We fed them baskets of kale, cabbage, comfrey and other greens along with the pellets. The meat is tender and good.

My Cub Scouts are learning to care for animals, skinning rabbits, and tanning the pelts. After doing so, the Cubs might not be able to eat 'Peter Cottontail,' but the experience may be valuable should food be scarce when they have children to feed.

Goat milk — The feed bill for goats is less than for cows in proportion to milk production, and they are safer around children. For several years we raised goats, drank the milk and made hard cheese with the surplus. For a time our young son's whole life centered around the goats—feeding, milking, and playing with them, and even sleeping in the loft of the small barn on nights the little kids were to be born. Our son and his friends barbecued young kids on a spit over an open fire and sold them back to us to get spending money.

Meticulous sanitary measures, prompt chilling and other factors that can be controlled, contribute to a milk product that anyone can learn to enjoy.

The most practical information on raising goats is from a 75-page booklet, "Dairy Goats—Breeding-Feeding Management," by Byron E. Colby, American Dairy Goat Association, Box 180, Spindal, North Carolina 28160.

Honey Bees — When people contemplate backyard beekeeping, many people shudder because of the natural fear they have of being stung. But this fear can be overcome, and you can learn to appreciate the fine family organization of a bee colony.

Eighty-two pounds of honey from one hive (with four supers) was a big surprise to a young couple in Utah the first summer they raised bees. During my first summer in the bee business, it was exciting to lift out two heavy frames of honeycomb and scoop it off to eat with a spoon.

My father, with his extended life of 94 years, has been involved with bee raising during his whole life. He still lectures at schools and colleges and has recently written a new book, *Bee Prepared With Honey* (Horizon Publishers and Distributors, Bountiful, Utah, $3.95).

The author's father, A. W. Andersen, age 94, capping honey.

Personal Aids

These personal aid ideas may seem rather primitive and time consuming for our modern day, but it is fun to have a youth by your side and experiment with whatever is available, forgetting the cares of the world.

Facial Care

—Honey facial: vigorously pat on face; rinse off.

—Milk mask to tighten skin and increase circulation: mix two tablespoons of dry milk and one tablespoon of water to a smooth paste; pat on face; dry and rinse off.

Fragrant Smells — Using oils is the easiest way to extract fragrant odors from plants. In a glass dish, put alternate layers of flower petals and cotton soaked in salad oil. Change the flowers every day until the cotton has absorbed a strong fragrance from the flowers. Press out the oil and put in small perfume bottles.

An excellent fixative and base for cosmetics is *orris root,* which can be obtained from any iris rhizome; the more fragrant the plant the better. Simply peel the brown outside layer as you would a potato. Slice the white inside part very thin and dry it in the sun until it is bone hard. Powder it in a blender or with a mortar and pestle. This fragrance becomes even more aromatic year after year. Add it to homemade cosmetics, according to the recipe or formula.

Toothpaste — Use equal amounts of salt and pulverized sage leaves for a tooth powder.

Hand lotion — The clear, thick liquid inside the aloa vera leaves is soothing. The thick jell scraped from a peeled stem of a comfrey stalk may also be used. A pinch of cornstarch or arrow root rubbed on the hands before washing keeps hands soft. Experiment with gluten water as a base for hand lotion.

Bath additives — Use a pound or two of herbs for a tea to pour into the bath water.

Insect repellents — Painted daisies (phyrethrum), dried and powdered, are one of man's oldest and safest insect killers.

Hair rinses — Brigham tea is an aid to restore color to hair. For light hair use a tea made from the blossoms of marigolds, mullein, yarrow. For darker hair, use elderberries, sage, burdock root or rosemary.

Deodorants and breath sweeteners — One family with nine children used lovage herb made into a tincture for both a mouth wash and a deodorant. Chlorophyll in comfrey, taken internally in adequate quantities, reduces or eliminates body and breath odors.

Ointments, Tinctures and Salves

An herbalist tutored me through the process of making wormwood ointment. (Space does not permit the details.) A friend brought me a bottle of his Plague Formula he had carefully made from 13 different ingredients. Ointments, tinctures, salves and syrups can all be made at home.

Salves

Following are two simple methods for making salves and ointments in the home:

1. **In the oven** — Place chopped herb in oven-ware dish or pan, cover these botanicals of your choice with melted lard, mutton tallow, goose grease or any pure grease (not drippings). Mix well and put in 200° oven until leaves, flowers, buds, etc., are crisp, usually 1-3 hours. Strain through a loose cotton cloth, seive or colander. Add beeswax which has been put in oven to melt so heated temperatures will be approximately the same.

Beeswax is included for the purpose of solidifying a salve or oint-ment. (About ½-1 ounce to 1 pound of lard.) When too much wax is added, the salve may set up quite firm, making it hard to apply on painful sores or scratches. Stir vigorously or whip with rotary beaters until cool. Beating action prevents a separation of the wax and fat. Spoon into jars and store in cool place as the fat will go rancid if kept too warm.

　　2. **On the stove** — Procedure is the same except the cooking process is accomplished by placing on top of stove over low heat. Need not cover pan. Stir occasionally.

　　CAUTION:　Aluminum ware should never be used for salve making.

　　Emollient herbs which are soothing and healing: comfrey leaves or root, plantain, marshmallow leaf and root, chickweed, slippery elm bark, quince seed, flaxseed meal, dog tooth violet, aloe, coltsfoot, alder, lungwort (antiseptic).

Shoes

I watched three women make sandles, dress shoes and boots at home in a very professional manner.

During the war, a Ger-man family, working by candlelight, made soles for shoes. They took scraps of cloth and made a small braided sole like you would make a braided rug.

I saw shoes that Cuban refugees had made from a leather purse. The soles were made from a heavy car mat. Even if we don't make shoes from the beginning, it would be good to know how to repair them and have the materials to do it with.

Home shoe repair.

Chapter 3

Let's Be Healthy

Preventive Measures

THE DAY WILL COME when good health will be a changed way of life for many people. Today we find a number of doctors who are shifting their emphasis away from the traditional medicine and surgery and focusing more on preventive medicine. Their objectives are to analyze what vitamins, minerals, and nutrients the body needs. Therapists and teachers in emotional structuring and behavioral genetics find people's health also improves by training and application of principles that synchronize personalities, minds and bodies.

The shortage of doctors and nurses and the high cost of professional care has caused many families to take more responsibility for their own health. It is my belief that we will be taxed to the limit physically and emotionally in times to come.

The doctor and patient work together as partners for health of the "total man." The body itself is the healer, but it often needs help to function properly. When it does, we will experience health and happiness. A doctor, talking at a Cub Scout pack meeting, said there were seven doctors of good health: Fresh Air, Rest, Sunshine, Good Food, Exercise, Water and Power of Mind.

A prominent businessman in Portland improved his eyesight and health by natural means, through his own efforts. He began by giving up tea, coffee, tobacco, liquor, white sugar, white flour and salt. His recovery was such a miracle to his wife that she wanted him to help all their sick friends get well. He said to her, "I'll help them. I'll do anything I can for them. I'll stay up nights researching and loaning them the books to read and work with them—on one condition only: that they *first* take the same route I did and give up the things I gave up."

H. R. Alsleben, M. D.; W. E. Shute, M. D.; and others have in their clinics sophisticated equipment and techniques unfamiliar to most of us. This equipment detects disorders in time to correct them. A friend who has a health service tested my husband and me for seven factors that showed the tendency we had toward certain health conditions. We were charted and told how to change the body chemistry so the body can heal itself. This is a preventive health measure that I certainly favor.

What Is Good Health?

The book, *The Will To Live,* by Arnold A. Hutschnecker, M.D., should be in every survival library. It is a re-education on what health is all about. He says this:

> Health is not a stable condition of soundness throughout, like a steel building on a concrete foundation. Health is a state of balance maintained by perpetual adjustments to forces from within and without. Through the years, the days, the hours, both waking and sleeping, we are steadily responding to the conditions of life, to hunger and food, to cold and heat, to fatigue and rest, to anger and pleasure. We must also deal with our ambitions and our fears, with jealousy, with grief, with feelings of inferiority, with defeats as well as victories, and with the inevitable acceptance of aging. Health depends on how well the individual as a whole can maintain balance through all these changes.

Where to Go for Help

My learning in the field of health is broader than my mother's, who died 50 years ago. When we were sick, mother found the answer to most of our problems from spiritual and religious sources, by going to her knees in prayer or by the laying on of hands. I can seek help from the same sources she did, but also from classes, conventions, magazines, books, tapes, slides, films, news media, and doctors at home and abroad.

I have a sprinkling of knowledge about acupuncture, transcendental meditation, astrology, reflexology, contact healing and related zone therapy, spot therapy and massage, psychosomatic medicine, biochemical testing, metabolic nutrition, thermography and time lapse photography (for early detection of disease), Kirlian photography (aura is seen), tranquilizing effects of music, homopathy, laetrile, DMSO, cybernetics, color therapy, iridology, personology, yoga, macrobiotics, sampaku, yin yan foods and many more.

A knowledge and acceptance of many of these may be a blessing to us. The danger, as I see it, is to place our faith in these *alone* and forget the help, guidance and comfort from a Higher Being who is aware of our individual needs. A well-known Utah doctor has this plaque on his wall: "The physician prescribes, but God heals."

We are all interested in new information—but some of the basic concepts of family health and care of the sick in the home need to be learned or relearned by many of us.

A world-renowned church educates its women in several family health courses. The first course covered such topics as:

—Understanding disease, cause resistance, immunity
—Personal hygiene, physical fitness, weight control
—Dental hygiene
—Home accident prevention
—Preventing social and emotional illness
—Fostering mental health

The second course covered caring for the sick in the home.

—Learning to recognize symptoms of illness and what course of action to take
—Ways to protect family members from contagious diseases
—Diet of a sick person
—Medication wisely used
—Cleanliness, comfort, and proper moving of an ill person
—Spiritual and emotional needs, rehabilitation
—Caring for aging family members

These and other courses to follow are invaluable in learning to take care of some of our own health needs.

Chapter 4

Emergency Preparedness

Heating Our Homes: Heaters, Stoves, Fuel and the Sun

THE THOUGHT OF BEING WITHOUT HEAT in the winter is unbearable to Americans accustomed to year-round temperature-controlled homes.[1] Alternate sources of heat and fuel need our consideration.

Heaters and Stoves

Portable gas heaters — If electricity went off, we could always carry small portable gas heaters from room to room. But obtaining and storing the right kind of gas has its limitations and drawbacks.

Wood and coal-burning stoves in all sizes are being installed in new homes and old alike. A stove uses far less fuel (for the amount of heat it puts out) than most fireplaces. For three years, while we were building our home, we heated five rooms

Wood and coal burning stoves are very practical and economical.

---

1. In Boston last winter one family reports their electrical bill was around $375.00 for one month, with the thermostat set at 68°, and with them wearing sweaters when they sat down to eat.

with our little 22-inch twilight stove. This little stove was then put into a corner as an antique. After 20 years we placed it in front of the fireplace with an asbestos board covering the opening. The stove pipe emptied into the fireplace flue through a hole in the board. With a recent addition of a new dining room, we have installed a simple white enamel wood burning range. If we had no other heat in the house, most of our activities would take place in this one room.

Before installing a wood-burning stove, check at the court house and see what the building codes are in your area. In our location, stove pipes have to be 12 to 18 inches from the wall, depending on the wall covering, and the stove 36 inches from wood or combustible material.

It isn't necessary to have a brick chimney. The stove pipe can go right up through the roof by using certain insulated approved metal chimneys. A two-story home in upper New York, built over 150 years ago, had the stove pipe from the first floor extend on through the bedrooms upstairs and out the roof. I'm sure the pipe gave off enough heat to take the chill off the rooms on cold winter nights.

Fuel — During the war a lady in Germany had to part with her embroidered tablecloth for a small bag of coal. For your peace of mind, be familiar with every conceivable type of burnable material in your area. Collect and store what you can.

Sawdust logs — We used four pressed sawdust logs a day at a cost of 68 cents during a 10-day experiment. These may be hard to get if the demand is great enough. Wood and coal might be scarce, too.

Chipboard — From a lumber yard, we bought damaged 4' x 8' chipboard sheets (compressed sawdust). Cabinet shops may have scraps. We cut this up in pieces narrower than the stove (so it wouldn't burn it out) and stacked them flat on top of each other. It burned slowly for a very long time.

Other Burnable Material:
—I saved all my *peach and apricot pits* to burn, and intend to make charcoal out of them. (See page 143, Volume 1, *Passport to Survival*)
—We could burn *corn cobs or dry bones.*
—In Louisiana, the small *pecans* that cover the ground and are too tedious to crack are used for fuel.
—Dried *stalks* from Jerusalem artichokes will burn.
—Store a pile of newspaper logs—soaked, twisted and dried.

—We may be twisting *hay* into a hard stick like Laura and Pa did in the book *The Hard Winter.* (*Little House* books by Laura Ingalls Wilder, pg. 189.)

Growing firewood — Those who have room might want to plant some trees for firewood. Alder, willow or maple are good. Alder in our area grows 20 to 30 feet in about five years and as big around as a man's leg.

Storing coal — Store coal in the dark away from air. (Air tends to break down coal into small pieces so it doesn't burn as long.) Small quantities can be stored in basements; or dig a hole outside, line it with plastic, fill with coal, and cover with plastic and dirt. (Normally you would need a ton per month for your fireplace.) One ingenious family in Utah has their coal supply stored under the front lawn.

Fire Starters:

—In India I saw neatly-tied bundles of small *limbs and twigs* (faggots) for sale in an open yard. As starters for open fires, these were a necessity. It provided young children with a job and kept the ground entirely clear of debris. (I was surprised to see, in a market near my home, small bundles of kindling wood for 75 cents.

Selling faggots (limbs and twigs) in India, as fire starters.

—Save all your *paper goods* (cups, containers and such) to start fires.

—Fill a quart screw-top jar with sawdust. Pour in as much fuel oil as the sawdust will absorb. Keep it tightly closed. A small quantity of this mixture will burn long enough to light even damp kindling.

—This summer I plan to collect a few sacks of *thistle down* for tinder.

—Using a *candle* to get fires started usually works.

—Put *steel wool* (00 size) between two flashlight batteries to create a spark and make the steel wool glow.

—One-fourth cup of *kerosene* thrown on paper and kindling before you strike the match is a good fire starter (but it seems dangerous to me).

Solar heat — My research on solar energy has been an interesting experience. The endless days of bright sunshine while in Australia was a contrast to our overcast skies in the Northwest. I learned that the sun is heating all the government houses in Australia's North Territory. There is no air, water or thermal pollution when we convert solar energy directly. It is comforting to know we have the sun from above for warmth, even if we run out of the fuels we have traditionally used.

In Albuquerque, New Mexico, Steve and Holly Baer live in a solar heated home. They used 90 steel 55-gallon drums filled with water heated by the sun inside a glass wall on the south side of their house. At the price of steel today it would cost a total of over $1,000 for the drums. Reluctantly, the plans for their heating system were deleted.

In a recent trip to Israel, I was surprised to find solar panels and cement water tanks on the roof of almost every private home.

Solar absorbers — A friend in California says the solar absorber he had installed on his roof saves over $10 a month on his fuel bill.[1]

Southern exposures — When the sun is low on the horizon in the winter, the rooms you want warmed by the sun must be on the south.

Expedient Winter Clothing

I am indebted to Cresson H. Kearny[2] for contributing information on emergency preparedness. His background on expedient winter clothing is extensive. He has lived, worked and slept outdoors under primitive conditions in cold areas—from the slushy, wet mountains of south-central China and Scotland to the dry, cold Andes of Peru and the Rockies. Among his friends are many experts on winter clothing. He has this to say about keeping warm:

―――――――

1. Sold by Solar Energy Systems, P. O. Box 711, Valley Center, California 92082.

2. The U. S. Atomic Energy Commission provides funding for the Civil Defense research (Health Physics Division) done by Mr. Kearny and his staff of Oakridge National Laboratory, Tennessee.

Good winter clothing can be improvised out of even ordinary city-type clothing and materials (mainly newspapers, towels, bedsheets and plastic) found in almost all American homes. In wearing this type of expedient clothing and footwear, I am sure that most Americans could work outdoors without injury at near-zero temperatures. If urban Americans wore their warmest available footwear while working or walking outdoors at near-zero temperatures, their feet would freeze in a few hours at most.

Warm feet — It is difficult to imagine a time when we would need to wrap our feet in newspapers to avoid frostbite. But for peace of mind I want the experience and know-how of keeping warm in any situation. My thoughts take wings as I envision Alaskan friends, miles from the city, needing shoes for cold feet (perhaps during an emergency when they were housing other families), or families moving from a hot climate to sub-zero weather, building a cabin in the mountains. Following the instructions for wrapping feet could prevent serious complications.

Who would think it possible to hike three miles in wet snow without shoes or boots and still have warm feet? This has been

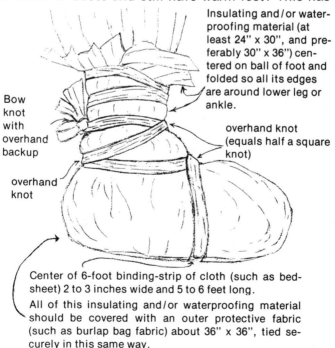

Insulating and/or water-proofing material (at least 24" x 30", and pre-ferably 30" x 36") centered on ball of foot and folded so all its edges are around lower leg or ankle.

Bow knot with overhand backup

overhand knot (equals half a square knot)

overhand knot

Center of 6-foot binding-strip of cloth (such as bedsheet) 2 to 3 inches wide and 5 to 6 feet long.

All of this insulating and/or waterproofing material should be covered with an outer protective fabric (such as burlap bag fabric) about 36" x 36", tied securely in this same way.

done by adequately insulating the whole body—especially the feet. Here is how Mr. Kearny does it:

Leg insulation:

—Over his leg, 10 double-page sheets of newspaper wrapped with their 24-inch width around his leg over the top of thin cotton pajamas.

—Tied above and below the knee, the newspapers were covered with thin cotton trousers.

Foot, ankle, and lower leg:

—A sock, covered with a polyethylene bread bag.

—This plastic bag was covered and held in place by a second thin sock.

—A rectangular 'insole' (one inch wider than Kearny's foot, and one inch longer) made of 10 double sheets of newspaper folded to produce an 'insole' 120 sheets thick.

Top of improvised shoe — After the leg is wrapped and two pair of stockings put on with a plastic bag in between and a thick newspaper insole, then...

—Stand on 10 double-page sheets of newspaper and draw them up around the foot and ankle so all the edges are above the ankle.

Tying on the shoe:

—Tie securely with a two-inch wide, six foot long strip of cotton bedsheet tied around the foot, ankle and lower leg (sandal-tie fashion).

—Use simple over-hand knots each time the foot or leg is encircled, and finish with a bow knot. (See sketch on page 31.)

Waterproofing:

—Use a 36" x 36" sheet of 4-mil. polyethylene secured with an identical strip of cotton bedsheet.

—For an outer protective covering it is best to use burlap bag fabric (34" x 36") tied with a third six-foot long strip of cotton bedsheet, tied around the foot, ankle and lower strip securing the loose edges.

Recap of materials needed:

newspapers	4 strips of cotton sheeting
2 pairs of socks	1 yard square of plastic
2 plastic bags	1 yard square of burlap

Testing the footwear — Mr. Kearny hiked at near zero temperature with the expedient footwear (just described) on one foot and the famous Korean War "Mickey Mouse" boot with sealed-in insulation on the other. Both feet were equally warm. Young test subjects, with better circulation, were almost too warm while hiking in the snow with this type of expedient foot covering.

Waterproofing light-weight shoes

—Put a plastic bag over your sock-covered foot and ankle before putting on shoes.

—Cover low shoes with two rough bath towels and

—a piece of 4-mil. polyethylene. (A piece of shower curtain will do.) Bring it up around the foot and leg so all the edges are above the ankle.

—Tie it with a six-foot strip of bedsheet, as in preceding instructions.

—Outside this waterproofing use a tough fabric for a protective covering. (Old drapery material will do.) Tie as before.

—As a test of effectiveness for this footwear, after the insulating material was securely tied, the waterproofed feet were dipped into ice water for about half a minute before the beginning of a one-hour hike in the snow. Feet remained dry and warm.

Keeping Warm at Night

It is possible to sleep comfortably indoors at freezing temperatures without blankets or winter clothing. This is done by insulating the whole body with newspapers, towels or bedsheets. These insulating materials must be placed under your clothing (even city-type clothing will do), and must be fastened securely on your head and feet. Properly protected in this fashion, you can even work outdoors without hardship at near-zero temperatures.

How insulation material keeps you warm:

—A sufficient thickness of insulating material traps air in thousands of very small spaces.

—The air remains trapped in these small spaces, but body moisture (water vapor) can move outward without dampening efficient body-insulating materials.

The best kind of insulating material to use:

—Use newspapers or ordinary brown paper on the outside with porous material underneath.

—Layers of any porous fabric covered with paper traps air.
—These materials allow very little air to escape, yet they permit body moisture (water vapor) to move outward through them and not dampen the clothing.
—Do not use coated or glazed paper (such as magazine paper) or any even semi-waterproofed material for body-insulating material except to keep *outside* water from penetrating.
—Down socks, vests and shirts are manufactured. A friend who wears them assured me they were worth the price.

Insulating all parts of your body:

—Be sure to insulate well the parts of your body that usually are poorly insulated—your head, neck, legs and hands. Remember to keep the ears well covered. Cold air in the ears causes a loss of balance which may cause you to fall when walking in cold weather.
—Remember that you cannot fully sense heat losses from your head and neck, although up to 30 percent of your body heat may be escaping from these areas.
—Also, remember that much body heat escapes from lightly clothed legs and bare hands.
—If all parts of your body are efficiently insulated, your feet and whole body will be warm with a minimum of insulating materials.

Avoid getting too warm:

—Before you get warm enough to feel sweat on any part of your body, take off and / or open up some clothing.
—The first and easiest steps to avoid getting too warm are to bare your head, neck, hands and wrists; then,
—Reduce the insulation over the chest and stomach.

Tests on keeping warm:

—Recent tests indicate persons occupying cold shelters for days would be warmer and more comfortable if clothed or shod so as to keep warm, rather than trying to keep warm by wrapping blankets around their bodies and legs, or trying to get under blankets.

Expedient winter head covering:

—Use two rough bath towels wound around the head and covered with a paper bag.

Sleeping in a trench:

—Mr. Kearny's two teen-age daughters slept in a trench shelter one January 10th. The inside temperature was 35°F when they entered the shelter.

—They slept on newspapers and on top of two thin cotton blankets spread on the dry, rocky floor.

—The girls kept warm by each wearing two towels over their heads, neck and shoulders and

—Over their bodies they wore girl's light underwear and 10 double-paged newspapers.

—Over each arm was worn a wrapping of eight sheets of double-paged newspaper.

—Over each leg, a wrapping of eight sheets of double-page newspaper was worn over lightweight cotton pajama bottoms, covered by a man's cotton trousers.

—Feet and lower legs were insulated with socks covered by two towels and a burlap bag, or by 10 double-page newspapers covered with bedsheet cloth or polyethylene.

If space permitted, I'm sure you would be interested in the details of Mr. Kearny living in homes in China in sub-zero weather without any heat whatsoever. The padded clothing on the babies made them look like roly poly balls. The details of the women doing their work were most fascinating.

Isometric exercise:

"Isometric exercises saved my life," one reader reports. "My bed was wet and snowy. I had no tent. It was a harrowing experience, but not too uncomfortable because I would awaken from the cold, exercise, glow from the warmth, drop off to sleep— repeatedly throughout the night."

—Isometric exercise applies to voluntary muscles that will contract for you.

—Beneath the skin's surface are many capillaries; as the muscles contract and relax, this forces warm blood to the surface. (Up to 50 times more.)

—Practice holding each contraction to the maximum intensity of which you are capable for a slow count of six.

—Try to contract (tighten) each muscle or group of muscles separately.

About space blankets:[1]

—A space blanket is made of five layers: plastic, aluminum, etc.
—Claims are that it is ten times warmer than wool, under wet outdoor conditions.
—Use like plastic, to keep outside water from penetrating.
—Use it to protect briefly against cold wind or around the body if sufficient paper or other windproof material (through which water vapor can pass) is lacking.
—Prolonged use of a space blanket as a bed cover, outside in near-zero temperature, caused the bedding under it to become very damp, which puzzled us until we realized body moisture could not escape.

Other Helps for Extreme Weather

Our skin helps us adjust to extremes of heat and cold.

—Shivering, for example, can produce heat approximately equivalent to running at a slow pace.
—Brushing the skin helps it function properly.
—One family with three children under seven years believes a romp in the snow in bathing suits keeps them strong. (Their skin gets accustomed to hot and cold.)

Vitamin C has a natural thermal or warming benefit for the body.

Canadian doctors have found that an increased amount of Vitamin C during the winter will help produce more natural body heat. "People exposed to chilly temperatures and whose food supply was limited have been found to develop disturbances in the circulation of their feet. Such problems could be relieved or avoided if these people were given extra ascorbic acid." Tests proved Vitamin C could offer protection against frostbite.[2]

Homes With and Without Air Conditioning

My daughter's electric bill in July in Houston, Texas, was over $50. Air conditioning in hot climates is a blessing at any

---

1. A space blanket, 84" x 56", weighs only 12 ounces and currently costs $6.97 in sport shops.

2. The theory is that with a Vitamin C deficiency, certain enzymes needed for stimulation of blood circulation cannot do their job.

price, but we may not always have it. Before air conditioning, several big cool, leafy shade trees shaded most every house in town. Porches on the north or east made for pleasant living and sleeping.

Harold Lloyd Wright, one of the world's most famous architects, built a house in the desert that was pleasant and cool without conventional air conditioning. To have comfortable homes in the future, we may all have to be Harold Lloyd Wrights and use our creative God-given talents.

If money or energy is scarce, I suggest the Kearny air pump (ventilating fan). Good air circulation and a gentle breeze may bring comfort to the sick or injured, young or old, under adverse conditions (such as when Mr. Kearny, a sick man, lay in a stifling hot Army hospital in Calcutta). An adequate supply of cooling outdoor air is essential to survival for those in a crowded fallout shelter.

Homemade Ventilating Pump

The Kearny Air Pump (or KAP) resembles a venetian blind in an open doorway, hinged at the top. The "flaps" are thin, *flexible* plastic. The device is pulled back and forth with a cord to pump large volumes of cooling outdoor air through a shelter and to fan the occupants of a shelter room. (See drawing and description.)

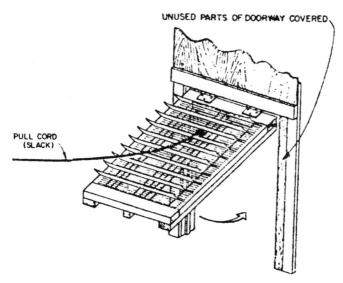

KAP in doorway (with flaps open during its return stroke).

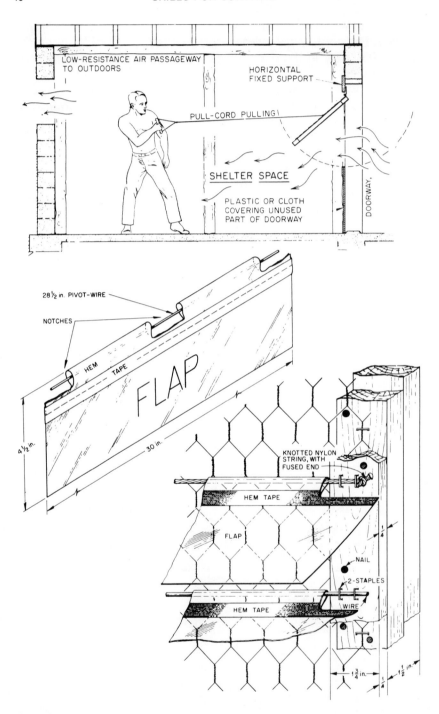

LOW-RESISTANCE AIR PASSAGEWAY TO OUTDOORS

HORIZONTAL FIXED SUPPORT

PULL-CORD PULLING

SHELTER SPACE

PLASTIC OR CLOTH COVERING UNUSED PART OF DOORWAY

DOORWAY

28½ in. PIVOT-WIRE

NOTCHES

HEM TAPE

FLAP

4½ in.

30 in.

KNOTTED NYLON STRING, WITH FUSED END

HEM TAPE

FLAP

NAIL

2-STAPLES

WIRE

HEM TAPE

1¾ in.

1½ in.

¼

In warm weather it is essential to pump large quantities of outside air through a crowded shelter to prevent the body heat produced by the occupants from raising the air temperatures in the shelter to dangerously high levels. In hot weather, many times as many persons could survive the heat in typical below-ground shelters through which adequate volumes of outdoor air are pumped than could survive in these same shelters if they lacked forced ventilation. Furthermore, you should realize that even in cold weather some outdoor air (about 3 cubic feet per minute [cfm] for each shelter occupant) must be pumped through many shelters, primarily to keep the carbon dioxide exhaled by shelter occupants from rising to harmful concentrations in the shelter air.

Ref: ORNL-TM-3916

Hot Weather Clothing

After being in a few "hot" spots in my life, I have some ob-servations to make:

I like to wear comfortable clothes no matter what job I'm doing. On a July afternoon it's hot in our attic, and I had the task of rearranging all the storage after a new floor was installed. I was dripping wet, but comfortable in my loose, coarse, white cotton lace jacket over short slacks. What's so bad, I reasoned, about plain, profuse, salty perspiration (with no odor, when we are eat-ing mostly raw salads and fruits)? As water leaves the body, it carries warmth along with it, and you feel cool if the air is dry enough and moving a little to evaporate the moisture.

I was comfortable in Thailand's hottest weather in a sturdy white cotton lace dress with a flared skirt that absorbed the mois-ture and showed no evidence of my being wet from the skin out. It was also hot when I arrived in Manila. People moved slowly in the heat of the day. During the cool early morning hours was the time to clean the sidewalks. I can still hear the swish, swish, of the big hand-tied brooms below the window of my upstairs YWCA room. A white peasant blouse and skirt were comfortable in the heat, but my first choice was the white lace.

But we're talking about survival, not white lace—

My daughter, on a 26-day survival hike, said the leaders wore buckskin shirts to protect them from both heat and cold. If they were near a stream in the heat of the day, they dipped their shirts in the water, returned them to their backs, and went on their way in cool comfort.

If the heat is unbearable, dig a trench at night to take a nap in the next afternoon. Be sure to have it face north and south.

A friend, who on several occasions experienced extreme temperatures of heat and cold, assured me that the discomfort didn't last forever. In two or two-and-a-half weeks he became acclimated.

Emergency Lights, Camp Stoves and Solar Ovens

It is wise to have more than one kind of emergency light in case fuel, mantles, chimneys or parts are not available for the particular lighting system you have.

Carbide lamps — Coal miners once used these, and they are again becoming popular as an emergency light. The fuel for them comes in pellets that lasts for years. The pellets form acetylene gas when water is added and are safer to store than some other fuels. The small size lamp costs about $8.00 (larger one $17.00), and pellets are $1.00 per pound.[1]

Aladdin lamps — These use kerosene and have a mantle (and a tall narrow chimney) that give off a bright light (100 watts). They cost around $30.00. The first night we used ours, we turned it low before leaving the house. On returning, we found the house full of black smoke. A little adjusting of the wick prevents this; so you need to be near to watch it.

A 'can lamp' [2] — This is a safe way to carry around a candle. a cross cut is made on the side of a tin can towards the back. The points are pressed to the inside, and a candle is pushed up part way through the hole. As it burns, twist the candle up farther into the can. A cord or wire is attached to both sides of the can for easy carrying. (See illustration on page 43.)

Bottle lamp — This lamp, using fats and oils[3] from the kitchen, is a safe emergency light. Most everyone would have a quart jar and some cooking oil on hand. (See illustrations on pages 43 and 44.)

Grease wick lamp — This is the most primitive form of light. A homemade wick is soaked in grease or drippings of any kind and laid in a pan or saucer. One end is then lit. A two-foot length

1. Andy and Bax Sport Shop, 324 S.E. Grand Avenue, Portland, Oregon 97214, carries these lamps; also Zicon, Inc., P.O. Box 9228, Millcreek Branch, Salt Lake City, Utah 84109.

2. "Roughing It Easy," Thomas, Dian; BYU Press, 1974, Provo, Utah.

3. Civil Defense Research Project, Kearny, C.H.; Oak Ridge National Laboratory.

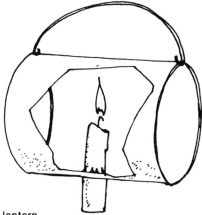

nail

Tin can lantern.

Loop to hang lamp
(large enough for finger)

To light lamp, first
make match longer
by taping or tying
it to a stick.
To extinguish, drip
oil on wick.

Attach aluminum foil
2/3 around jar and under
its bottom and to wires
to act as a reflector
(not illustrated)

Light wire

Clean glass jar
free of labels

Flame from end
of wick is just
above oil surface

Fill jar no more
than half-full
with cooking oil
or fat

A fine wire tied in
its center around
the nails, with the
ends of the wire
wound in opposite
directions around
the cotton-string
wick. Use cotton
that is slightly less than 1/8-in.
in diameter. Use window screen
wire or other
equally fine wire.

Bent nail, tied
over top of another
bent nail, so the
base will not rock

Use nails about ½-in.
shorter than the
diameter of jar

Keep extra wire and
wick-string in shelter

Wire-stiffened-wick lamp

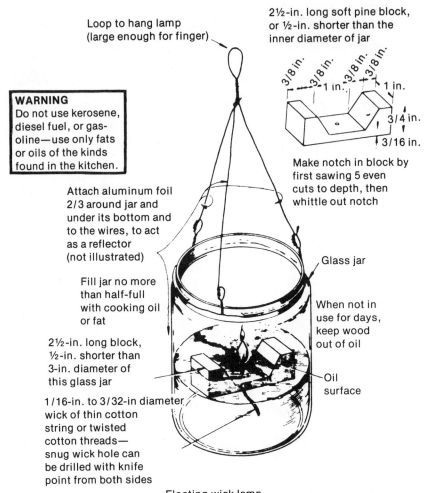

Loop to hang lamp
(large enough for finger)

2½-in. long soft pine block,
or ½-in. shorter than the
inner diameter of jar

3/8 in.   3/8 in.   3/8 in.   3/8 in.

1 in.   1 in.

3/4 in.

3/16 in.

WARNING
Do not use kerosene,
diesel fuel, or gas-
oline—use only fats
or oils of the kinds
found in the kitchen.

Make notch in block by
first sawing 5 even
cuts to depth, then
whittle out notch

Attach aluminum foil
2/3 around jar and
under its bottom and
to the wires, to act
as a reflector
(not illustrated)

Glass jar

Fill jar no more
than half-full
with cooking oil
or fat

When not in
use for days,
keep wood
out of oil

2½-in. long block,
½-in. shorter than
3-in. diameter of
this glass jar

Oil
surface

1/16-in. to 3/32-in diameter
wick of thin cotton
string or twisted
cotton threads—
snug wick hole can
be drilled with knife
point from both sides

Floating wick lamp

will last only an hour, however. To make the wick, use strips of
cotton material 1/2 inch wide. Twist *tightly*. Fold in half and twist
in opposite direction. Twisting gives the wick body. This type of
wick can also be used when dipping candles.

For a ten-day period, we lived under simulated emergency
conditions and turned off the utilities. I enjoyed the various types
of lights we used instead of the sameness of our usual ones. I
also felt the urge to get things done during the daylight hours.
Things quieted down when night time came (as it should). Why
not burn a grease wick lamp while reading pioneer stories to the
children for added interest?

Simple stoves — To warm a little milk for the baby:
—Take a #2 (or tall) juice can.
—Punch holes all around the can with an ice pick, about every inch.
—Cut the two ends off the can.
—Purchase cans of canned heat sterno or wood alcohol.
—Light the canned heat and place the prepared can over the fuel.
—Place a pot or container on top of the can.

"Buddy burners" have been used for some time by Boy and Girl Scouts and could be used at home in an emergency.
—Use a gallon can with the bottom cut out and about five holes punched in the sides with a can opener towards the top and the bottom.
—Cut a door about four inches wide and one and one-half inches high and bend upwards.
—Wind strips of corrugated paper around a tuna can to the height of the can and pour wax over the paper, filling the can.
—Use this as a burner under the bigger can. Eggs and bacon can be fried directly on the top of the can.

Solar oven — If no fuel or electricity were available, we could still bake our bread and cook our food in a solar oven. The test

A solar oven.

oven in the preceding illustration reached a temperature of 350 degrees in 15 minutes. This was in Arizona in mid-January, with the air temperature in the low 60's. The first time it was used, it

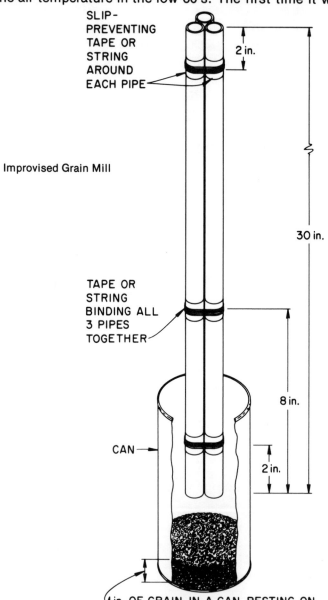

SLIP-
PREVENTING
TAPE OR
STRING
AROUND
EACH PIPE

2 in.

Improvised Grain Mill

30 in.

TAPE OR
STRING
BINDING ALL
3 PIPES
TOGETHER

8 in.

CAN

2 in.

1 in. OF GRAIN IN A CAN RESTING ON
A HARD, SMOOTH, SOLID SURFACE

baked a loaf of bread in just over an hour. A whole meal can be cooked in the solar oven.

The oven shown is a simple galvanized iron insulated box to hold the food, with a tilted glass in front and metal reflectors on the side to admit and trap heat inside the box. The oven door is at the back.

Grinding Grain

Electric grain mills are widely sold today. However, if you or your neighbors or friends don't have a mill and you have wheat stored and need some flour, try Mr. Kearn's invention for pounding the grain. It works, but I'm thankful for other ways to do the job.

- —As long as we have electricity, I will use my grain mill, blender and small seed grinder.
- —Without electricity, I would depend on our large old-fashioned coffee grinder or a small square one we take camping, or the heavy duty hand grinder similar to a meat grinder.

An interesting report is of hearing the din in the early morning hours of African women daily pounding their millet with a mortar and pestle.

Emergency Foot-Powered Drive Unit

During a large scale prolonged power failure, we would find ourselves becoming more and more dependent upon the only dependable power source in existence—our arms and legs.

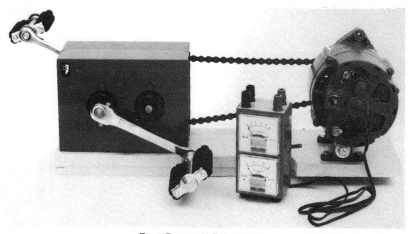

Foot Powered Drive Unit

The drive unit shown on page 47 is designed to allow you to use your feet to drive several different items that normally require electric power. By hooking an electric generator to it you can generate up to 75 watts of power at a normal cruising speed. This electric power can be used to drive C.B. radio stations, television sets, etc. Small rechargeable lantern batteries can be recharged and used for portable lighting, etc. Other non-electrical items such as food and tool grinders, forge and heater blowers, can also be driven.

Emergency Drinking Water by Distillation

Those who have attempted to store sufficient drinking water to last a year or more realize the impracticality of such an attempt. Using only five gallons per day, we would require room for over 1,800 gallons. This amount would weigh eight tons and occupy 250 cubic feet.

The only answer is to be able to purify almost any water that can be found. There are many methods for obtaining drinkable water from polluted water. The four basic ones are: *chemical treatment, filtration, freezing,* and *distillation.*

Chemical treatment such as halazone does not remove the particulate matter (which could be radioactive from atomic fall-out), and the taste leaves a lot to be desired. The small activated charcoal/silver filters now on the market also will not remove all particulates and contaminants.

Of all the methods used to purify water, distillation is the simplest and most practical in an emergency. In the method described in this article we simply boil the polluted water, condense the resulting steam in a long copper pipe and collect the water in a glass container of some kind. In the process everything is removed from the water and it is perfectly clean, provided the condenser pipe and collector were clean to start with. Also, there can be no volatile oils, solvents or iodine present in the polluted water or fractional distillation which will contaminate the distilled water. If plastic containers are used to collect the water, there is a chance of some objectionable chemicals being released from the plastic because of the heat.

Being such a good solvent, water can contain an endless number of things. In polluted water we often find such disease germs as dysentery, typhoid, cholera, etc. These germs give us the most important reason for purifying the water before we drink it. Other things such as pesticides, oils, solvents, clay and sand sediments, detergents, sulphur, salts, vegetable matter, nitrates, and radioactive particles can be dangerous and should also be of concern.

From the standpoint of construction, cost and available materials, the system shown has proven to be the simplest and most practical. A five gallon metal container for the boiler, a long piece of copper water pipe or fin heater tubing (10 feet or more) for a condenser, and a glass container to collect the water is all that is needed to distill up to 10 gallons of water in a 24 hour period. Assemble as shown in the diagram.

A simple and practical method of water distillation.

OPERATION

1. Fill the boiler (metal container) with about three gallons of contaminated water. *Warning:* Do not use water that has oils or solvents in it.

2. Screw the metal cap on the boiler and place the small marble over the hole in the cap as a safety valve.

3. Place the copper water pipe in the hole in the side of the boiler and wedge a rag around it to seal it.

4. Build a good hot fire under the boiler and bring the water to a boil.

5. Permit the water to boil for about 10 minutes and let the distilled water run out on the ground. This will help vent off any unwanted gasses or odors.

6. Now place the glass collecting container under the pipe end.

7. Aeration of the distilled water should be a matter of practice. Adding air to water removes odors, gasses and the flat taste. This can be accomplished by pouring the distilled water from one clean, wide mouth, glass container to another through the open air. Repeat this several times. Glass jars, for example, work very well.

8. If odor or bad taste still persists, then you will have to find another source of water.

9. The boiler should be rinsed out each time it is used if radioactivity in the water is suspected.

10. With normal caution the distillation of water by this method should be no more dangerous than ordinary cooking.

If the fuel to boil the water is scarce, then constructing a solar still is a good alternative. Several types are described in a book called *Direct Use of the Sun's Energy* by F. Daniels.

In a recent class on behavioural genetics I sat deep in thought over the need for good drinking water in times of stress. Our lesson was on signs of strain, and use of adrenalin. Adrenalin increases our native capacity to perform, which can be an advantage, however it is a drug or astringent and to control the negative effects of prolonged use of adrenalin it helps to increase our liquid intake and get more rest. (Rest may not be possible, but hopefully good drinking water will be available.)

Water Storage and Conservation

Alternate Sources of Water Supply

As we reach higher levels of family preparedness, it is wise to consider an alternate source of water should city water fail. During one of the last California earthquakes, a family of eight living in Granada Hills found the drinking water they had stored in gallon jars was soon gone. They went five days without any running water in the house. What could they do should this happen again?

Here are eleven suggestions:

1. Store water in every empty *bottle* you have. Purify with eight drops bleach solution to a gallon of clear water. (See "Water for Survival," *Passport to Survival,* Chapter 11.)

2. A unique invention for water storage, which I saw in Boulder, Colorado,[1] was *40 gallon units* made of heavy polyethylene that interlocked, one stacked on top of the other. One hundred sixty gallons of water could be stored in a 38" x 14" floor space.

3. Many homes have durable 1,000 gallon capacity *fiberglas storage tanks* buried in the ground.[2] A few years ago we were considering a fiberglas tank holding 3,000 gallons. It was six feet in diameter and sixteen feet long and installed at a cost of $1,200.

4. *A private well* seemed to be the answer until I found out you needed a permit and $1,500 or so. In some counties, no more permits are issued. My brother and several other home owners in his neighborhood in Danville, California, dug a 20-foot well for about $300. (They hit water at 10 feet.) A half-horse power motor brings up a steady stream of water that is used to water the garden and keep the lawns green, at a cost of about 50 cents a day. Water is rationed in their area—225 gallons a day for inside and outside use.

5. Water shares for gardens once were sold with almost every city lot in Utah. We can no longer depend on this source of water.

6. A *cistern* seemed a logical place for water storage. A man near me dug a hole in the ground fifteen feet square and twenty feet deep. He lined it with cement and it now holds 3,000 gallons. A cement contractor gave me an estimate of between $3,500 and

---

1. Blaine Robbins, 4615 Macky Way, Boulder, Colorado 80303.
2. Lynwil Industries, 3065 West 21st South, Salt Lake City, Utah 84119.

With interlocking 40-gallon units, 160 gallons of water
can be stored in a minimum of space.

$4,500 to build one like it! (That was the price or our new five-room home some years ago.)

7. A plastic *swimming pool* fifteen feet in diameter holds 5,500 gallons of water and costs about $160.00.

8. Users of *water beds* consider this a good emergency water supply. You can store 90 gallons in a twin size bed, 135 gallons in a queen size bed and 175 gallons in a king size bed.

9. For ten days we used water from a *rain barrel.* Water from the roof filled the 55-gallon drum in two hours in a light drizzly rain. We had a downspout from the gutter to the holder. The oil drum was cleaned with solvent, scrubbed, then coated with metal primer and a coat of black asphalt enamel. The outside was painted the color of the house. Netting could be stretched over the barrel to keep the water clean and free of possible mosquito breeding in the summer, and the water could be distilled if it were necessary.

10. A simple device to pull water up out of the well, if electricity went off was invented by an ingenious man.

11. *Wind mill*—Claims are that you can generate electricity from the wind by using a vertical instead of horizontal blade that will turn with the wind from any direction—No tower needed to draw water from underground.[1]

Rain water from roof filled this 55-gallon drum in two hours.

1. Order—"Manual of Individual Water Supply Systems," U. S. Documents, Government Printing Office, Washington, D. C. 20402. Price: 60 cents.

Note: See "Getting Water Out of the Ground," "Passport to Survival," page 129. The plastic sheet used over the vegetation in the hole in the ground works better if it is Dupont's "Tedlar Plastic." (Some plastics drip straight, missing the container at the lowest point.)

Washday

Keeping Clean With a Minimum of Water

It is said that embattled soldiers can brush their teeth, make their coffee and take a bath using a single helmet full of water.

I saw a demonstration of washing your hands in a cup of water—lathering and rinsing twice.

In the summer, bathe the children out on the lawn at night before going to bed. One family used a hose that was connected to a barrel of water on a black painted roof. The sun heated the water.

When bathing in a basin of water, even cold water, wash from face down to feet, rubbing on a little water at a time. In humid, hot weather, washing too often with soap and water removes natural skin oils and also may encourage skin infections. Rinsing off with plain water several times a day, like jungle natives, helps keep skin healthy.

Sweating in a sauna bath[1] and then using a little water to rinse, saves water. While visiting Larry Dean Olson's campground in Montana, I was interested in the sweat shelter a man had built near a stream that he and his two children had used the night before.

It was dome-shaped, covered with canvas, held up with flexible limbs tied together and anchored in the ground. Sleeping bags were thrown over the top to keep the heat in when he was using it. Red hot rocks heated in a fire outside the shelter were brought inside with a shovel. From a teakettle he poured mullein tea on the rocks. (That helped clear up his son's congested nose.) They left the hot, steamy shelter a few times to rinse off in the stream and then rushed back in to get warm. If they weren't near a stream, they would have poured a little water on each other to rinse off.

Other Tips for Saving Water and Fuel

New products and inventions to save water and fuel are flooding the market. News media, magazines and pamphlets bring to the public ingenious ideas.

Trying to conserve water during 17 days in August while taking care of four grandchildren wasn't easy. There were more clothes, dishes, hands and windows to wash. Too much water was used when they washed the car, sprayed the walks, took a bath, or rinsed out the garbage cans. To break the habit of wasting water will take time. (I even tried wiping the dust off the car with a dry cloth instead of squirting it with the hose—looked good.)

Flushing toilets—During our ten-day experiment with our water turned off, we flushed the toilet by pouring two or more gallons of water from the rain barrel (dish or mop water) into the toilet bowl.

Wash day—If we would cease hot water laundering of clothes, we could save 300,000 barrels of oil a day, according to a recent study presented to the U. S. Treasury Department. (1/74 National Food and Farming Magazine)

A family in Montana this past summer washed clothes in cold water in an electric washer on a platform under a tree, and hung the clothes on lines to dry.

---

1. See "Outdoor Survival Skills," p. 10, for directions for an earthen-covered sweat lodge shelter.

One Minnesota housewife that didn't have a water heater in the house, pulled her washer out on the porch, filled it with water and heated it with a doughnut shaped heating element on a handle. Batch after batch of light clothes, dark clothes and then rugs were washed in the same water.

One mother I know washes four loads of laundry a day, seven days a week. She has six children.

Families in the past have kept clean without such an extravagant use of water and power. Dark fabrics, detachable white collars or fresh aprons were customary.

Improvised water tap—Use a gallon bleach bottle. Punch a hole with an ice pick in the side two inches from the bottom. Use a golf tee for a cork. Fill it with water, it will not leak out until you unscrew the lid and remove the cork.[1] (Use as an overhead shower.)

Homes Away from Home

Home Underground

The underground shelter is far from new in history. In the early 1600's, they were being used here in America long before the log cabin was introduced. Many sod huts and river bank shelters were left along the pioneer trails to the west. From the standpoint of durability and ease of construction, they have no equal. As far as tools and supplies are concerned, they require little more than a shovel and some sturdy poles or logs.

Last spring my husband established a new emergency shelter underground. We left our home with eight suitcases, about eight bags (with sturdy handles), sleeping bags, air matresses, provisions for lights, food and water, and waste disposal. Our underground home was 15 x 4½ x 6 feet deep. It was covered with two-by-fours and plastic.

The bags contained such items as a radio, tape recorder, socks to darn, knitting, embroidery work, a song book, other reading material, foot massage supplies, nuts to crack and capsules to fill. The suitcases with the food, clothes and supplies mentioned in Chapter 1, now have been repacked, labeled and are stored behind my Oriental screen.

This was a humbling, creative experience. Our abode was pretty, clean, comfortable and quiet, but without such a wide

---

1. "Roughing It Easy," Dian Thomas, Brigham Young University Press, pp. 36 and 974.

Home away from home—underground.

choice of what to eat, wear or do as we normally enjoy. It was a time to get to know ourselves and each other better. "Be It Ever So Humble, There's No Place Like Home" is a song we didn't sing, but should have. I thought many times of our grandparents who lived with their four children in a dugout in Mayfield, Utah, 100 years ago, during the winter.

Tree House Home

I recently saw a circular tree house with shake siding and a shingle roof built in a tall fir tree about two feet in diameter and 20 feet off the ground. It had windows and a door and front porch. A ladder leading up to the house was hinged at the top with a rope fastened to it to pull it up.

To get down to the ground quickly, there was a one-inch rope over a pair of pullies. A 100# weight was attached at the other end as a counter balance. The rope had a big knot in it at the top. One could open the front door, quickly step out on a porch, grab the knot, and ride down to the ground.

Electricty, water and waste lines were all inclosed in a shingle-covered box on one side of the tree which did not detract from the appearance of the tree. A small wood-burning stove was used to keep warm. A septic tank was ready to be put in the ground.

Heavy furniture or supplies were lifted up through a large opening (in a glass covered dome). Heavy things were pulled up with a hand-operated wench. Part of the wench was a plywood wheel about four feet in diameter with ornamental hand holes.

The interior was home-like, with hanging plants and a tree trunk and branches (with the bark peeled off) where things were hanging.

The employment of used and discarded materials made it an inexpensive home. I understand they cannot tax a tree house. I don't know how they get around the building code.

Earthen-built Homes

I just returned from visiting an adobe brick home owned by my grandparents that has been standing for about 100 years. (We read of dirt buildings standing today after weathering over 4,000 years.)

A friend brought me a packet[1] of information about a special material called Rub-R-Slate (R.R.S.). It is much lighter than cement stucco that has been used to coat adobe houses. It is tougher, will stay on longer and keep water out. R.R.S., to be used with clay, etc., is obtainable from contractors who do streets, driveways, etc. R.R.S. is an excellent low-cost floor covering. It is termite-, rat-, and rot-proof and fire-resistant; no wood need be used.

With R.R.S. you can plaster the whole inside of the room—walls, ceilings and floors. It leaves no cracks for dirt, germs or filth—making the whole easy to clean. The room is warmer. The floor is restful to the feet and nerves. The whole room is tight as a jug.

R.R.S. and adobe or clay can be used to construct:

plants	root cellars	incinerators
shops	churches	septic tanks
schools	swimming pools	old building repairs
storage sheds	fish ponds	
barns	garden pools	

I was impressed with the comforting thought that corn cobs could even be crammed into ten-inch-thick forms for a very warm wall. The cobs were first sprayed to keep down decay bacteria. Studs were set in as needed and wire netting nailed to them to keep the cobs in place. Rub-R-Slate would be put on over this with a towel, old broom or spray gun.

There are also other building materials which are exciting to think of using:

—Ground up cardboard and clay
—Peat moss blocks
—Hay and corn cobs tramped in forms
—Cemented burlap bags on a wire like a clothesline plastered over with R.R.S.
—Plastic bubble homes and furnishings may become common in the future.

Some think if lower-cost building is not soon found, the common man will have to quit living in houses as we know them today. (A garage costing $7,000 was constructed recently in my area.) For the past two decades there has been a tendency for a *car* to take first place in the hearts of Americans, crowding out

1. Write Bays Laboratory, Cedaredge, Colorado 81413, for "Nuway Building—Build Better for Less—Much Less," by Jack Bays.

home to second place. I believe that this tendency will be reversed and that in the future people will spend more time making their homes more attractive or liveable. Let's keep our "ear to the ground" for ways to provide shelter for people in the future when life as we know it today may fade away.

Atomic Warfare

As I move onto a higher level of family preparedness I want to be prepared to live through a nuclear war. As Russian military strength continues to increase, the need for individual civil defense preparations become more apparent. I have long felt the need for personal preparation in this area. Six personal reasons why I want the experience of living through a simulated nuclear war are:

1. I want to be able to face every possible event in my life with dignity and inner peace.

2. I want to assume a personal responsibility for my welfare in times of disaster, to the best of my ability. This lightens the load of government.

3. I hope to lift the fear and gloom many have by sharing my preparation experiences.

4. This higher learning experience will prepare me to better cope and adapt, and be flexible in the future (to "roll with the punches").

5. It will add a new dimension to my present lifestyle and responsibilities.

6. I want to graduate from this learning experience and "register for a new class" to give me further peace of mind.

Threat of Nuclear War is Real

Our past and present goal of getting a year's supply of food and necessities and of preparing for such emergencies as earthquakes, floods, tornadoes, droughts, and plagues, seems enough without adding the nuclear threat. Yet my research convinces me that that threat is real!

Four reasons why:

1. Because we deserve it, as crime, immorality and desecration of the Sabbath increase. The people of America who fail to serve God can expect to be chastised and humbled by whatever

means Deity chooses. A prophet has written, "This is a land choice above all other lands. Wherefore he that doth possess it shall serve God or shall be swept off." (Ether 2:10-12.)

2. Soon wars will end and we will build, plant, harvest, learn, love and serve in peace as many of our fears vanish. But until that day comes, any of several countries in the world could instigate a nuclear war, and world-wide fallout could be a threat to us all.

3. The momentum is increasing in preparing for nuclear war, especially in the Soviet Union. Factories and grain silos are underground, population shelters are blast proof, and fall-out proof shelters protect military equipment. Troops exist. The calculation that 98 percent of the Soviet population could survive a nuclear attack[1] is based on a scenario in which the Soviet people, directed by Altunin and 78 generals, would leave the cities and strike out across the countryside, carrying shovels to dig their own shelters, approximately three days before the U.S.S.R. instigated a nuclear war.

4. Under a Socialistic regime, the job of government preparedness is simplified where there is public ownership of land, houses, enterprises and utility service. Recent news articles repeatedly assert that the United States is not keeping pace. So, the free agency we still have carries a responsibility for the citizens of this choice land to personally prepare. And yet, we have studied this threat very little. We don't prepare because we don't know what to do. It is unfamiliar to us. Noah and his family learned new skills and built the ark that took them to safety while others scoffed at the idea. When a crisis comes, the time of preparation is passed!

Seven Ways I Can Prepare on the Home Front

1. I can learn enough about atomic warfare to carry within my skull a reasonably accurate (even if gross) image of what life will be like. War is an unfamiliar territory for a housewife. (It is very hard for me to even write down what I have learned. I escape to the garden to plant some peas, or go bake some bread or wax a floor. A happier experience than writing about war would be to learn to use my new spinning wheel.)

1. ..."Kremlin leadership no longer accepts the theory that no nation could survive a major nuclear war and they are preparing to survive. It also follows they no longer accept the theory that any nuclear war is unthinkable...The United States would lose 57 per cent of its total population...Soviet Union would lose 2 per cent." ("Spotlight," March 28, 1977.)

I am sure with young children, you think there is no time to prepare; but as parents responsible for lives, we may have to take the time.

2. Knowing what to do lifts the gloom and despair of such a disaster. Begin talking to your family about a shelter you can use as protection from trans-Pacific fallout as well as from blasts and heat. (As you study, read swiftly over the accounts of great blasts from bombs over the city and the hazards of the blast downwind, intense heat.) Most of the things we worry about never happen anyway.

Your children will respond to building a "fort," surrounding yourself with a few feet of concrete, earth, water or wood in your house.

3. Now that we have rehearsed the scenario of nuclear warfare and taken action making plans for a fallout shelter, we now can collect what provisions we need for a three-day minimum stay in our shelter. Use four *sturdy* suitcases.

> A. Put in some food, comprising a reasonably balanced diet for the family. (Rotate this, restocking every year.) Include supplements.
>
> B. Include two or more changes of clothing for each family member for hot and cold weather.
>
> C. Prepare a first aid case. The Russian's individual standard first aid packet contains anti-radiation tablets and anti-vomiting tablets (potassium, iodine and etaperasin). Iodine tablets or capsules should be included.[1] Old, clean sheets to tear for bandages for future use would occupy small hands.
>
> D. Assemble things to do—books, records, tape recorders, transister radios, harmonica, fiddle, whittling knife and wood, sewing and pictures. (Have a tape recording of birds singing.) In some container or location, assemble things like bedding, foam pads, waste disposal for young and old, flashlights, stove, dishes and pans, a thick carpet runner for comfort, and a hand wheat grinder (coffee grinder).

4. If you are going to dig your own underground shelter and have the experience of living in it for three days, some advanced

---

1. I am told that the United States is making a mistake by not stockpiling a larger quantity of iodine salts; and if the body has enough iodine, radio-active iodine from fallout will not be absorbed by the body.

planning will make the experience more enjoyable. Have on hand boards or logs for the roof. Construct a ventilating pump so the air can be changed every hour in your shelter. You will need large and small plastic bags and a garden hose for water. (See directions for constructing a shelter.)

5. Physical as well as mental health will play a big part in how well you survive the "rehearsals" or the real experience. Your body is a powerful fighting system. Your natural body defenses can handle radioactive fallout particles as they do any other thing that damages your body, providing, of course, that you do not take damage faster than it can be repaired. Fortunately, we do have certain foods—like alginate (abundant in kelp), pectates from pectin in fruits and vegetables, bone meal and dolomite supplements—that give us some protection from the absorption of radioactive materials in the blood stream. However, they must be taken in the right amounts.

6. Build a fall-out meter. Kressen Kearney has worked out a tested do-it-yourself fall-out meter. People with no more than an eighth grade education can make it out of ordinary materials.

7. Now, we have learned about nuclear war, made plans for a fall-out shelter, and stocked it with necessities. We have practiced digging an underground shelter and living in it. We are working toward optimum physical health. Now the seventh way we can prepare is a "rummage table" of ideas including developing more patience, love, keeping order in our homes, and having deep faith in a Higher Being. We also need to be planning our days so that our short term and long range goals are met.

I keep thinking of the siege of Leningrad. They were an unprepared people. Librarians answered thousands of questions put to them by both military and civil authorities about such things as: how to make matches, candles, yeast, soap, artificial vitamins, flint and steel lighters. Grain, meat, sugar, lard and butter for the city had been stored in wooden buildings—very little was stored in people's pantries. Flames and smoke reached thousands of feet over the city when the Germans set fire to the food warehouses; now it was all lost. Teen-agers died because of the inequality in the rations. They needed as much food as the workers.

We can become a prepared people. Even though such cities as Portland report that they have fall-out shelters for the entire population, I prefer to provide my own.

Emergency Underground Shelter

The shelter described later in this chapter was designed primarily as an atomic radiation shelter by the Oak Ridge National Labs in Tennessee. A family of six plus a pet dog lived comfortably in this shelter for a period of 3½ days without coming out. Additions made by the family such as window screens, plastic walls and floor covering, a carpet, a privacy curtain, a water-sealed toilet, a wash area and several other items made it far more livable.

The experiment was sponsored by the Oak Ridge National Labs in August of 1974 to see if it was feasable for an average family to evacuate a city with nothing more than what they could carry in or on top of their automobile and be dug within 24 to 36 hours from the time of notification. The father of the family felt that it could have been done in half the time if there were a strong fear incentive. The father was a 44-year-old office worker and no longer accustomed to hard physical labor.

Figure 1 shows a plan for laying out the basic shelter, while figure 2 shows a cross section of the shelter after it has been dug. The depth of 4½ feet left no standing room for an adult except for a small "stand hole" dug at one end of the shelter. The reason for digging no deeper than this becomes quite apparent after you

Fig. 1

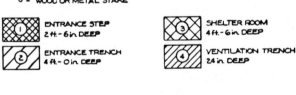

0 = WOOD OR METAL STAKE

ENTRANCE STEP 2 ft.-6 in. DEEP

ENTRANCE TRENCH 4 ft.-0 in. DEEP

SHELTER ROOM 4 ft.-6 in. DEEP

VENTILATION TRENCH 24 in. DEEP

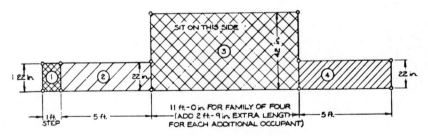

SIT ON THIS SIDE

11 ft.-0 in. FOR FAMILY OF FOUR
(ADD 2 ft.-9 in. EXTRA LENGTH FOR EACH ADDITIONAL OCCUPANT)

1 ft. STEP · 5 ft. · 5 ft.

22 in.

PLAN FOR STAKING OUT TRENCH ON TOP OF GROUND
(SEE LEGEND FOR 4 DIFFERENT DEPTHS OF TRENCH)

Fig. 2

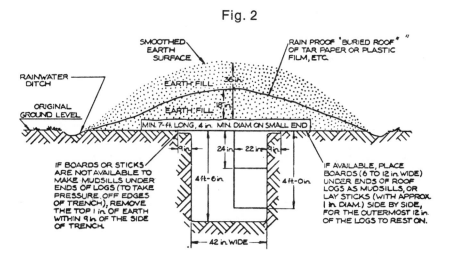

SMOOTHED EARTH SURFACE

RAIN PROOF "BURIED ROOF" OF TAR PAPER OR PLASTIC FILM, ETC.

RAINWATER DITCH

ORIGINAL GROUND LEVEL

EARTH FILL 36 in.

EARTH FILL 18 in.

MIN. 7-ft. LONG, 4 in. MIN. DIAM. ON SMALL END

IF BOARDS OR STICKS ARE NOT AVAILABLE TO MAKE MUDSILLS UNDER ENDS OF LOGS (TO TAKE PRESSURE OFF EDGES OF TRENCH), REMOVE THE TOP 1 in. OF EARTH WITHIN 9 in. OF THE SIDE OF TRENCH.

IF AVAILABLE, PLACE BOARDS (6 TO 12 in. WIDE) UNDER ENDS OF ROOF LOGS AS MUDSILLS, OR LAY STICKS (WITH APPROX. 1 in. DIAM.) SIDE BY SIDE, FOR THE OUTERMOST 12 in. OF THE LOGS TO REST ON.

9 in. — 24 in. — 22 in. — 9 in.

4 ft-6 in.   4 ft-0 in.

42 in. WIDE

CROSS SECTION THROUGH
WIDTH OF TRENCH SHELTER

try it. Digging just a few inches beyond 4½ feet becomes almost as difficult as digging the first two or three feet because you have to lift the dirt above your shoulders and throw it over the pile at the edge of the hole. The 42-inch width was sufficient to give a little leg room and passageway. The length of 2½ feet per person worked out just right in our case. It may be a little discomforting to realize that the depth is more shallow than a standard grave and the width is just exactly the same. At one time we had three visiting observers in the shelter with us which made a total of eight adults and one child. You could build an underground fortress or castle if you had the time and strength, but we had neither in this experiment.

Figure 3 shows the plan for laying logs over the top of the shelter. Bed sheets were laid over the logs to keep out the dirt that was piled on top. It's absolutely necessary to cut back the top edge of the wall a foot or so and a few inches down in order to remove the roof weight stress from the edge of the wall which could cause it to cave in. Note the plastic bags that are cut open and hung from the top of the wall to prevent us from getting dirt all over when we rubbed against the wall. This worked very well. Later, plastic bags were also placed on the floor with a scrap piece of rug laid over that for the length of the shelter. We had no

Fig. 4

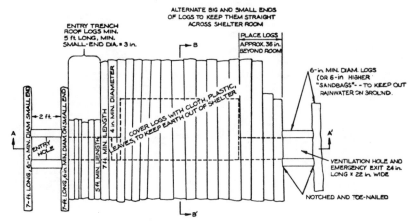

ROOF LOGS = MINIMUM 7-ft. LONG, 4-in. MINIMUM DIAMETER ON SMALL END
LAID ABOUT 2 ft. PAST EACH END OF SHELTER ROOM.

PLAN VIEW OF TOP OF SHELTER- SHOWING PLACEMENT
OF LOGS FOR ROOF-EARTH FILL NOT SHOWN

Fig. 3

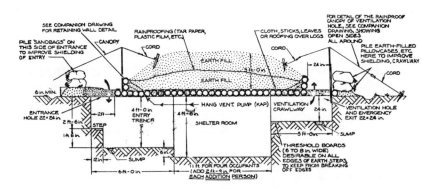

CROSS SECTION THROUGH
LENGTH OF TRENCH SHELTER

problems with dirt getting into anything for the entire length of our stay.

A cutaway drawing of the shelter is shown in figure 4. On the left is the entry tunnel with the "KAP" air ventilation pump suspended from the overhead logs. This pump is made from plastic strips attached to some coat hanger wires and is an extremely efficient high air volume pump. Without this pump, it would have been impossible to remain below ground for more than an hour in our situation. The air in this shelter must be changed with the pump at least every hour or two, as carbon dioxide settles toward the floor.

A bunk bed was made up of 3/4 inch plywood and boxes. Folded sleeping bags were used as mattresses, which proved to be satisfactory, but not nearly as comfortable as the "bedsheet hammocks" which we were shown how to construct after a day or so of using the bunks.

Chairs or a bench may be used to sit on while two persons are sleeping. Care must be taken to avoid cutting off leg circulation when sitting for long periods of time. The same sheets which are used to make the hammocks can also be used to make a very comfortable chair. With wall-to-wall carpet you can use the floor as a living or play space for children.

A curtain suspended from the log roof is a blanket and is used to provide privacy. When not in use, it is tied back against the wall. An adult can stand in the "stand hole" (shown in figure 5) which allows them to stretch from time to time. The toilet seat is mounted on a piece of 3/4 inch plywood. Three five-gallon pails with the bottoms cut out are stacked up to form a pit for the toilet. This is water sealed, odorless and took no more than 45 minutes to construct and install right on the site. A five-gallon bucket is used for washing dishes and clothes. With a plastic bag in it, it can be used for sponge bathing very easily. The water supply for washing and flushing the toilet came from a pit dug near the shelter. This pit was lined with plastic and held 50 gallons of water. This is the quantity we used during our three and one-half day stay with no conservation efforts. A garden hose coiled up in the sunshine provided us with hot and cold running water. A simple siphon arrangement gave us the necessary water flow and acted as an indicator of the water level in the pit. For water buckets, we were shown how to use pillow cases lined with plastic bags. Two of them could be carried quite easily.

The small tunnel on the right serves as an air exhaust and an emergency exit. It is covered with an old window screen to

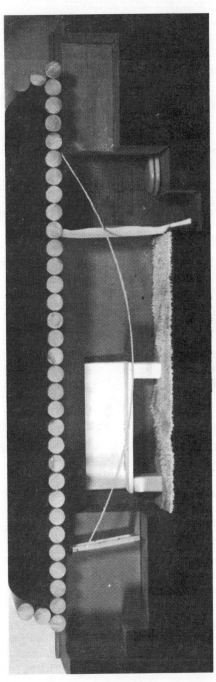

Cutaway Model
Fig. 5

keep insects from coming in. Insects collect around the air exhaust area and very few around the entry tunnel. The fact that a person knows he can escape through the emergency tunnel if he has to, will serve to eliminate the panic of claustrophobia which occurs in most people when they feel closed in. We also found it absolutely necessary to keep a small homemade cooking oil lamp burning in the exhaust tunnel to provide orientation when in the dark.

If this experiment serves no other purpose, it has proven to us that living under such austere conditions with your family is not the nightmare I at first thought it might turn out to be, but rather an experience which we as a family look back on as a very pleasant, fun memory.

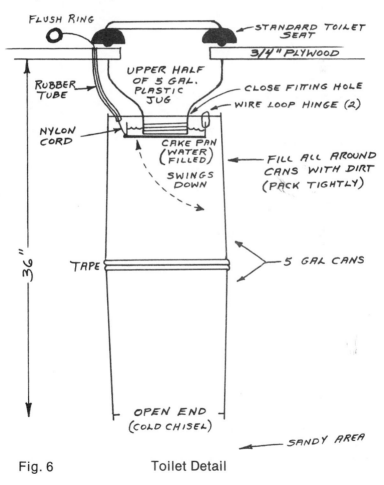

Fig. 6   Toilet Detail

Part II

Better Home Gardens

Thankful for the fall harvest.

Chapter 5

Where to Plant Food Crops When You Think There's No Place to Plant

WE ARE COMING TO A SECTION NOW, more pleasant to think about, which could also be a "passport to survival." Fortunately, more people each year are choosing to live simpler, more natural lives, centered around the production of their own food. It seems home gardening is here to stay. We don't all have space for long straight garden rows, but don't give up.

Seeds Grow in Out-of-the-Way Places

In emergency situations, seeds can be planted in restricted areas such as

—In open sections between brick, concrete or wood paving.

—Around storage sheds, boulders or in unplowed fields.

—Along fences, walks, river banks or train tracks.

—At the foot of a tall green hedge or behind and between flowers.

—Flat against a wall.

—On a raft at anchor on a pond (so the deer can't get near).

Containers Can be Most Anything That Holds Soil

A variety of items can be used to hold soil for planting purposes:

—Plants are happy in baskets, boxes, buckets or barrels, sitting on steps, balconies, flat roofs or terraces.

—Plants grow in wheelbarrows, oil drums or in old washing machines on legs.

—Food crops can grow in hanging baskets, inside or outside.

—Plant indoors in bottles, lids and pans.
—Use any room in the house, including basements, attics or garages.
—Grapes will grow in redwood planters 33 inches high and 16 inches square with an overhead frame to guide the vines.

Various Beds and Environments

Seeds accommodate us by growing in various beds and environments such as:
—Pyramid beds for more planting surface.
—Three-tiered raised beds, like stair steps with fencing on the top, for tall crops.

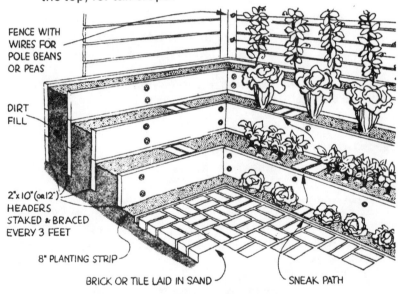

FENCE WITH WIRES FOR POLE BEANS OR PEAS

DIRT FILL

2"x10"(or 12") HEADERS STAKED & BRACED EVERY 3 FEET

8" PLANTING STRIP

BRICK OR TILE LAID IN SAND

SNEAK PATH

Three-tiered raised bed.

—Raised beds with fertile soil[1] shoveled right over the top of heavy clay or adobe soil. (Earthworms will help mix the two together.)
—Jumbo truck tires filled with soil.
—Table height beds for wheelchair patients.

_____

1. If there is no other source of fertile soil, see custom-made soil formulas in the book, "More Food From Your Garden," by J. R. Mittleider.

—Window boxes. (I gardened in one for 20 years in a south bay window. It was six feet long, 24 inches wide and 18 inches deep. Vegetables among the potted plants are decorative. I've seen growing boxes taller than a refrigerator with inside shelves and special growing lamps.)

—Greenhouses can be two or three feet high, or giant inflated plastic greenhouses covering 4,600 square feet like those in Tucson, Arizona, Arabia, and elsewhere.

Food Crops on Campuses, in Parks, on Rented Land

In Switzerland, fruit producing trees are planted as shade trees. In vacant lots or unused areas, fruit trees are planted for the use of all. You would never see a Chinese Elm, for instance, or a purely ornamental tree. The trees must serve three purposes: shade, food, beauty.

Some day when food is extremely scarce, we may suffer remorse over the acres of meticuously kept landscapes on college campuses that could have been planted to fruit trees and food crops[1]—food needed for health of body and mind by students far from home on limited budgets.

I marveled at the beauty of food crops on a visit to the 450-acre botanical gardens in Whitnall Park in Wisconsin.

There is an increase of "people's" gardens in many cities. In one locality a fruit tree can be rented for about $30 a year. The family prunes the trees in the spring, picnics under them in the summer, and gathers the fruit in the fall.

Through the train window in Europe, I saw large sections of land divided into small rented garden spots (each with a tool shed with curtains at the window), where people from the city came to plant and harvest. Riding the train to Pikes Peak in Hong Kong, I saw pitifully small grave-sized gardens along the tracks.

In El Salvador a garden is planted behind the church. A family there loosened the soil with a grubbing hoe. To make a rake, they drove long nails through a block of wood.

If we want to grow food crops, we usually find a way.

---

1. On a college campus I recently passed a row of double flowering crab apple trees heavily laden with beautiful fruit. Wax wing birds feast on them after the first frost, I am told. Homeowners pick the fruit for jelly.

Chapter 6

Working With
the Soil

Soil Conditioning and Planting in One Day

NORMALLY IT TAKES THREE OR FOUR YEARS to get poor soil in good condition.[1] But, if you wake up some morning determined to have seeds in the ground before nightfall, here's one way to do it:

1. Decide on a sunny location for your garden.

2. The soil should be loose and fluffy so plant roots will have easy access to food and water. "But it's hard baked clay," you say; "I can barely nick it with a spading fork."

3. Keep nicking here and there and then go rent a tiller to finish the job. (The nicks will provide toeholds for tiller tines.) If the ground is too hard to even nick with a pick—sorry about that; you cannot plant today. Soak the soil and wait—maybe two or three days—for the soil to be the right dryness to till.

4. Do not start paying rent on a tiller until you have collected enough organic material to cover the area three feet deep and to be worked into the soil a layer at a time. This amount to a beginner sounds unrealistic. What you use for this three foot high layer of loose material depends on what is available locally. My friend in California uses rice hulls, buckwheat hulls, peanut shells and coffee grounds (from a coffee factory), none of which I find in the northwest. But, we do have grass and leaves. If I cannot beg or borrow enough of these, I may have to buy some sawdust, peat moss, hay, straw or steer manure in a bag and maybe some sand.

---

1. For more soil conditioning information, read Chapter 3, page 13, in the book, "Organic Method Primer," by Bargyla and Gylver Rateaver.

Of course, if you have a big compost pile all decomposed and ready to spread on the land, so much the better.

5. Now you have the tiller and the organic material. Go over the bare land with the tiller three to six times to get a loose layer at least three inches thick.

6. Spread the loose material several inches thick and till three times. Add another layer and till again, repeating until it is all used up.

7. This uncomposted material has a tendency to make the soil acid, so a little ground-up agricultural limestone should be cultivated into the soil.

8. Your soil is now about half organic material and it needs nitrogen right away to help it decompose (especially if you have used sawdust).

A. Spray the soil with fish emulsion, manure tea, or add bone meal, blood meal, clover, alfalfa meal, chicken manure or hair from the barber shop—all high in nitrogen. The liquids are best as they are instantly available.

B. Or use a commercially prepared bacterial culture (used when making composts to hasten decomposition).

C. Or you might want to buy earthworms—500 or more of them. Turn them loose over the soil and let them chew away at the organic material and eliminate it. (Their castings are five times higher in nitrogen than the material they eat.)

Now after all these details, fuss, bother, work and expense you can forget about sticky mud and clods. Soon you will have soil you can dig with your hands and brush off, leaving them clean.

So far we have (a) tilled the bare ground, (b) tilled under organic material, (c) sweetened the soil with limestone, and (d) added some high nitrogen material.

Now we rake it smooth and give it a good deep soaking. If you want an "instant" garden, go buy a flat of vegetable plants: lettuce, parsley, green onions and the like. But mulch around them and shield from the sun if the weather is hot. In the meantime, soak your carrot and beet seeds to be planted later.

Soon your heart will be gladdened and your body nourished by food from your own garden.

Know the Soil

Real Soil

One writer, that knows the soil, describes it this way:

> It isn't real soil if you can't enjoy walking over it bare-
> foot, however tender your feet are. It isn't real soil if you can't
> scoop it up in handfuls effortlessly. It isn't real soil if you
> have to spade it up to make it loose...real soil is spongy and
> springy when you walk on it. Real soil will make a compact
> ball when you squeeze it in your hand, but crumble apart at
> a touch. Real soil you can dig with your hands and you can
> punch your closed fist right through it. When you brush off
> your hands, it leaves them clean. All you need of such stuff
> is one acre to grow all you want for yourself and your fam-
> ily.[1]

Minerals

One hundred and two mineral elements are found in the soil.
Familiar ones are calcium, phosphorous, iron, magnesium, etc.
(It is interesting that some of the same minerals in a shovel of soil
are found in bones, tissue and blood of man.)
Minerals originate in rock, which since time began are con-
stantly being broken down into soil.

Organic Matter—Humus, Water and Air

Organic matter and humus are sometimes thought of as one
and the same—but they are not. Organic (as pertaining to the
soil) means both plant and animal matter, dead or alive. As ad-
vanced decay of organic matter takes place, it is called humus.
   —The more humus in soil (15% is ideal), the more food there
      will be for bacteria and other soil organisms.
   —More decay will take place.
   —More nitrogen will be in the soil, which has a beneficial
      effect on plant growth.
   —The prime benefit of decaying material to the soil is short
      lived.

---

1. "Organic Method Primer," page 22, Rateaver.

As decay continues, we no longer have light loose bits of material ventilating and holding moisture in our soils, encouraging plant root growth. The humus gets old and disintegrates into minute particles and forms one of the 102 mineral elements in the soil. It is then in a more stable form than in its younger, fast-decaying period.

When humus is depleted, the soil gets tight so no air circulates. Air in the soil encourages bacteria and fungus organisms. Sufficient air is necessary for many soil processes to take place. If we want our soils to hold water, add humus. Humus holds water like a sponge.

Too much water allows the release of soil nitrogen. It also forces air out of the soil, which may result in sour acid soil. Too much air speeds nitrogen release beyond the capacity of plants to use it.

Replenish the Earth

Composts

We had beginner's luck with the first compost pile we ever made years ago in California. It was a learning experience for the children as we worked together collecting all the materials. They watched with interest as the steam poured out of the holes in the pile (made by poles) and later examined the miracle of rough smelly garbage and manure that was transformed into sweet smelling earth.

Some friends in Seattle attribute the highly-productive yield of their small garden to a Compostumbler that converts raw garden and kitchen waste into rich compost in 14 days. It sells for $229.

There are other ways of returning waste products to the land to replenish the earth besides making compost heaps, such as the following:

Use a blender or grinder — In one family a regular job for the children, after every meal, was to put all table scraps and vegetable wastes in the blender with a little water and pour the liquid on a designated spot in the garden. Use a hand grinder if a blender is not available.

Bury the garbage — Dig a trench about 15 inches deep and about a foot wide for kitchen garbage, cover with six inches of dirt. After a year plant peas or other crops in that area. A handicapped friend dug shallow holes with a shovel and buried the table scraps daily.

Bury such things as old sweaters, leather shoes and purses, furs, woolen pants and feather pillows. Put these in the bottom of a deep hole with a little soil on top before planting your fruit trees.

Bags and boxes — Big plastic bags can hold layers of garbage, fertilizer, soil and green material. Moisten, tie tightly and hang in the garage. Or, just put the garbage in the bag and lay it out in the hot sun, turning a few times a week.

Compost can be made in a row of boxes in the garage. Fill one at a time with layers of vegetable wastes alternately with rich garden loam, moisten and put plastic over the box.

Fertilizers — I once thought all chemicals were bad and anything organic was good. E. H. Bixby in his book, *Your Friend and Mine,* writes this about chemicals:

> Don't condemn them. They are taken from the soil and should be called soil balancing elements. They cannot cause damage *if they are needed in the soil.* The damage comes when we guess at what and how much to use in our soil.

So-called chemical fertilizers were developed when manure became scarce. Most of these combine natural rock bases with additions of soluble chemicals. For example, superphosphate is a natural phosphate rock treated with sulphuric acid to make it more soluble. This makes it available quickly to plants, but the accumulation of acids in the soil will certainly have adverse effects on soil processes.

Chapter 7

Important Plants

Many Types of Plants Needed

I'M PLANNING A "PERSONAL INTERVIEW" with every plant on my place. If plants don't have several good uses, chances are they will be replaced with ones that do. The changes and planting we do now may be to our advantage later on. We may need:
—More food for ourselves and others, for our pets and animals.
—Herbs to season our plain grains and legumes.
—Roots, leaves and flowers for our beverages.
—Sweet juice from sorghum cane we can grow in our gardens.
—Healing and medicinal plants for comfort and relief.
—Plants to help other plants grow and ward off insects.

Plants and Trees Have Many Uses

Plants and trees fulfill many varied purposes:
—Plants feed the soil when they are returned to the earth.
—We get firewood from the alder trees we had the forethought to plant.
—We have trees for shade from the scorching sun.
—There are plants that give us silky fiber to twist into cardage or to weave and wear.
—Some enjoy plants for decorative arts and crafts and family fun.
—Broom straw planted to make our brooms with as they do in Germany and other countries.

Bountiful harvest. (Photo - Gresham Outlook)

--We can use roots of the madder plant for red dye (to color Easter eggs), anise for licorice flavoring, milkweeds for soft padding, flowers for perfumes, and other plants for antiseptics, deodorants, lotions, abrasives and detergents. (Some of these uses are impractical, time-consuming and primitive perhaps, but for the "young in heart," it's fun to experiment.)

I expect to see food crops get priority in the future where space is limited. I would first plant:

Beets	Parsley
Carrots	Tomatoes
Green Peppers	Potatoes[1]
Onions	

For plant protein, Vitamin A, C, and Calcium (that storage grains are low in), I would grow:

Comfrey	Turnips (for the tops)
Mustard Greens	Dandelions
Kale	Alfalfa

---

1. See "Reader's Digest," December 1976, page 205, "Praise the Potato," the world's most important vegetable.

Vitamin A is also found in deep orange fruits and vegetables and in other dark green leafy vegetables like cantaloupes, papaya, yams, carrots, winter squash, broccoli, spinach, chard.

Three Plants to Supplement Our Grains

Comfrey

Comfrey is a fast growing green plant. It is an excellent food and a great aid to health, not only for man but animals and the soil as well. Every home needs comfrey.

Comfrey has been known to herbalists for about 2,000 years. There are 20 types of comfrey. Bocking 4 and 14 surpass the others. A new type with smoother leaves and very few flowers has been developed.

Comfrey is valuable as a low cost plant protein. What the world needs is a method of extracting the 3½ tons a year of pure protein that exists in a 100-ton-per-acre crop.[1]

Four essential amino acides in comfrey are: Methionine, tryptophane, lysine and isoleucine. If we were living mainly on wheat, beans, and legumes that are low in these amino acids, we would have a better protein balance by using comfrey. Comfrey contains almost twice as much more protein in the spring than in the fall. Certain varieties are higher in protein than others.

Using Comfrey as a Food
—Use the fresh tender leaves for green drinks, in salads, soup or cooked greens (White shoots under the soil are tender also).
—In the winter, use dry leaves for tea, or grind the dried root and leaves into flour. Use them in vegetable broth, soup or baked goods. Comfrey is rather tasteless and does not alter the flavor of other foods mixed with it. (In using green flour, you may need to find ways to disguise the color.)
—Avoid heating comfrey over 125°, as higher temperatures tend to destroy the allantoin and vitamins.
—A conference speaker and his wife from Japan take 100 grams of green comfrey a day in tablet form.

Comfrey as an Aid to Better Health — Allantoin is found in the roots of comfrey in the winter and goes up into the stem and leaves in early spring.

---

1. Hills, Lawrence D., "Comfrey—Fodder, Food and Remedy," New York, 1976, Universe Books, 381 Park Avenue South, N.Y. 10016, page 177.

Allantoin is a crystalline substance that primarily induces healthy new tissue growth by causing the cells of our skin, flesh or bones to grow and divide more quickly. It also has the ability to remove the undesirable necrotic tissue and clean up an injured area.

—The use of comfrey poultices hastened my recovery from an accident in 1974 that nearly took my life.
—Be cautious in using a fresh unheated poultice on open wounds. It is not an antiseptic. Don't hasten the growth of new tissue over a dirty wound.
—Comfrey salves, tinctures, and ointments are used.
—Comfrey is a potent source of chlorophyll with a similar structure to blood.
—A book[1] on medicinal herbs gives 30 uses for comfrey and how to prepare it for coughs, colds, burns, cuts and wounds, anemia and headaches, etc.

Comfrey as a Deodorant
—Taken internally it eliminates body and breath odors. One test reduced detectable underarm odors from 50 to 100 percent in all five patients within seven hours and was effective as long as 18 hours in dosages of 65 mg to 200 mg.

Comfrey as a Soil Builder
—Comfrey is a substitute for animal manure in the compost pile and in the soil due to its high nitrogen and potash content. Many gardeners cut the green leaves and bury them three to five inches deep and plant immediately over the top. Use about a pound of comfrey per foot of row. Use also as a mulch. (We are putting it around all our fruit trees.)

Comfrey for Animals
—Comfrey has been fed with excellent results to horses, cows, pigs, chickens, rabbits, geese and goats, as well as elephants and other animals at the zoo. It should be cut for animals before the flower buds appear, as animals do not like the large stems that develop. It can be dried for hay or fed green. It is a preventive and curative for scours and does not cause bloat. Comfrey-fed chickens in my area start laying sooner after being in a molt.

---

1. Kadans, Joseph N.D., Ph.D., "Encyclopedia of Medicinal Herbs," 1970, New York, Arco Publishing Company, Inc., 219 Park Avenue South, New York, N.Y. 10008.

Planting Comfrey

—Establish a permanent place for comfrey to grow. You shouldn't have to plant it again for ten or twenty years. Allow room to divide and transplant the roots. We started with one plant and now have 50. This green leafy, fast-growing plant grows about two or three feet high. The tap root goes down about eight feet for water and trace minerals. It likes moist conditions, but can adapt to dryer climates. Comfrey can stand frosts 40 below zero.

If a friend doesn't give you a root cutting, order one from a seed catalogue or store. Space the plants eighteen inches apart in the row. Cover with three inches of soil.

Brown spots on the leaves show a need for more nitrogen in the soil and more frequent harvesting of the leaves. Cut about every month during the growing season, two or three inches from the ground.

Alfalfa

In the spring of 1847 in the Salt Lake Valley about 2,000 destitute hungry pioneers gathered lucerne to eat (English name for alfalfa). Journals tell how they thrived on cooked greens to go with their stored grains and what an agreeable sensation it was to have their stomachs full.

If case history repeats itself and we are hungry when spring comes, I wanted to have alfalfa in my garden, so I planted a few rows. Last March when the weather was still cloudy, cold and wet, the only green things in the garden were the small green leaves on the crowns of the alfalfa and comfrey plants. I knew I would soon have enough for green drinks.

My family has been using alfalfa in tea and tablet form for over 40 years. Now it is routine to grow sprouts almost the year round for sandwiches and salads.

My research shows that alfalfa is a good source of Vitamin A, calcium and iron. Using the green leaves in green drinks (as soon as they are cut) helps preserve the valuable oil solubles. The enzymes in the green leaves aid digestion. Alfalfa tea has been used by many nursing mothers to increase their milk supply. Alfalfa tablets has relieved the pain of arthritis.

Alfalfa is a heavy feeder and needs good neutral soil. The roots go deep into the subsoil, five or ten feet or more, and pick up minerals often not found in worn out topsoil. Alfalfa, like other legumes, has the power to pull nitrogen primarily out of the soil. As a result it makes a good activator for the compost heap or helps garbage in the ground to decompose faster.

Jerusalem Artichokes

My neighbor had two acres of Jerusalem artichokes on his dry land farm in Montana. One spring about 38 years ago, grasshoppers by the thousands moved in over the land. They ate everything growing on top of the ground, except the stickery artichoke plants. Without this plant, he said, the family, the dairy herd, the pigs and chickens would have starved to death during the summer.

I consider my rows of Jerusalem artichokes as a stand-by emergency fresh vegetable supply. They are a potato-like tuber that stays firm and crisp in the ground all winter.

At a church pot luck dinner during the Christmas holidays, I brought a big platter piled high with slices of raw artichokes. They disappeared like melting snow. People didn't know if they were turnips or what—but those on diets were happy for something fresh to cut down on calories. (To prevent discoloration after cutting, soak in vinegar water—2 tablespoons vinegar to 1 quart of water—or use lemon juice or citric acid.)

They are referred to as "sunchokes" and sold as a specialty crop in the produce section of many food markets. They have 22 calories per pound, are 100 percent starchless, and contain calcium, Vitamin A and iron.

The leafy big plant grows about ten feet tall. The stems are hollow inside, and when dried out, they are tough and strong enough to use for garden stakes or fences. Just plant like you would potatoes. A new smooth American variety is said to be on the market.

Jerusalem artichokes are added as an important survival plant, because like comfrey and alfalfa they are a perennial plant that withstands frost. They are easy to grow and are a good balance for the grains we have stored.

Sprouting Seeds and Growing Greens

Growing Cereal Grasses

Buckwheat "lettuce," sunflower greens, wheat grass, garden cress and other greens can be grown in any shallow container you have (even a plastic lined box lid).

Cereal grasses can be grown in any shallow container.

Planting Buckwheat "Lettuce" in a Tray

1. Use unhulled seeds (not buckwheat groats). Soak two-thirds cup seeds (for a 12-inch square tray) for 15 hours. Drain and keep in a dark place until the seeds begin to sprout.

2. Mix equal parts peat moss (or compost) and garden loam in a plastic bag, dampen it, knead it and pour it in the tray to a depth of one and one-half inches. Roll it out or pat it down, moving the soil away from the edge of the container for better drainage.

3. Spread the seeds evenly on the surface. Cover with eight thicknesses of wet newspaper, then a plastic sheet to prevent drying.

4. After about three days, remove plastic and newspaper and grow in a light room for about a week, watering only when necessary.

5. The leaves (lettuce) are ready to add to a tossed salad when they free themselves from the seed, unfold and take on a bright green color; the stem can be used, too. Cut with scissors near the base.

6. After the harvest, break up the sod, dampen it, and allow it to disintegrate for future plantings. Compost starter will hasten the transformation of roots into the soil.

(*Note:* Plant wheat, sunflower seeds and even mung beans the same way. A sprinkle of soil over the sunflower seeds works best. Either hulled or unhulled seeds can be used.)

Planting Tips

—In order to expedite in-door planting, planning and organization of supplies are necessary.

—Establish a planting area and a growing area. Bring a bucket of soil in before the ground freezes over. Have a bucket for the sod to decompose in. Have your trays, plastic and newspaper in one place with some planting seeds nearby.

—If mold appears on the flats, the soil may be too wet or warm, especially for wheat. It is a cold weather plant. A fungus growth may be transferred from trays or lids of plastic re-used in planting. (To sterilize such containers or plastic, wash in chlorine water, one teaspoon to a quart of water.)

Growing Cereal Grasses — The following suggestions will explain how to sprout cereal grasses such as wheat, rye, oats, corn, barley and sudan grass.

1. Soak 3/4 cup of seeds for 24 hours.
2. Put 2 inches of soil in roasting pans.
3. Spread seeds.
4. Cover with 1/2 inch dirt and a wet porous cloth.
5. On 5th day remove cloth.
6. By the 7th night joint swells.
7. At 4 a.m., harvest.
8. Cut 1/2 inch above soil.
9. Refrigerate only 3 days.
10. Juice in grass juicer—pollution free.
11. Make delicious salads.
12. Replant every 3 days.
13. Grow in sun, plastic or greenhouse cover.

Scientific research has been done on growing grasses. The reason for using only the first blade growth is that the second blades produce a more bitter chlorophyll which, in the opinion of Dr. Thomas, contains but about 40% of the nutrients present in the first growth.[1]

The greatest potency from chlorophyll extracted from wheat grass is up to three hours after cutting.[2]

---

1. Christopher, J.R., "School of Natural Healing," p. 546.
2. Ibid., p. 547.

Wheat Grass — I plant wheat the same as buckwheat and have shown them to over 200 audiences. I have often carried a big tray of greens on the plane, fitting it under my seat. I watched these and other greens and sprouts being grown and used at Hippocrates Health Institute in Boston. Ann Wigmore, D. D. founder and director of the institute, has received world wide acclaim for her work.

The green chlorophyll is extracted from the grass with an electric grinder (a meat grinder can be used). It is sipped from small glasses; or when large amounts are needed, it is given through the rectum in an enema bag, retaining it for about twenty minutes.

A medical doctor I contacted could see no harm whatever in using the wheat grass for a food or a medicine.[1] He did not dispute the claims of Dr. Ann Wigmore that:
- —Chlorophyll enters the blood immediately when taken as described and rebuilds the red blood cells.
- —It is useful as a prevention and cure, especially for high blood pressure, liver problems, heart conditions and to prevent hemorrhaging.
- —It is useful as an eyewash, for toothaches and pyorrhea.
- —It miraculously repairs tissue.
- —Chlorophyll contains important B and C vitamins, enzymes and protein, as well as calcium, phosphorus, magnesium, sodium and potassium.

Sprouting the Seeds

Long Mung Bean Sprouts — Long, crisp, white sprouts can be home-grown if five rules are observed: darkness, water, drainage, warmth and a weight on top.
- —Tall, round, stainless steel commercial sprouters with one container inside the other and drainage in both of them are ideal. An improvised one can be made from two plastic containers with holes punched in the bottom.
- —Soften the beans by first rinsing in hot water and then keeping them under cool water for twenty-four hours.

---

1. Most doctors today subscribe to the magazine, "Nutrition Today." My doctor contact suggested information on wheat grass be sent to them for research and a possible article.

—Pour the beans in the inside container. They need room to
expand so an inch of beans on the bottom is enough.

—Cover the beans with several folds of burlap. This keeps
the light out, keeps them warm and holds in the moisture.

—Now put a bag of rocks over the burlap. The sprouts need
the resistance to grow thicker and firmer. One experiment
I made was unbelievable: a half pound of beans lifted
seven pounds of rock to the top of a gallon container in
five days. (But have pity on them—three and one-half
pounds are enough.)

—Run water over the beans every two or three hours.

Tips: Grow them at room temperature, with no light (do not
peek under the burlap). It takes water to grow about an inch a day.
They will have shaggy roots, green leaves, brownish color and
taste strong if these rules are disregarded. After about five days,
plunge the beans into cold water to wash off the hull. They are
now ready to enjoy, either raw or cooked.

Alfalfa Sprouts — My friend who owns the Sprout House in
Portland has 700 to 800 glass gallon jars of sprouts growing all
the time. Having the proper amount of moisture and drainage are
two tricks of the trade.

—Put two tablespoons of alfalfa seed and one-half cup of
warm water in a two quart jar. In about twelve hours rinse
and drain.

—Roll the seeds around the sides of a dry jar.

—Keep in a dark place at room temperature.

—When the seeds have started to sprout, look a little dry,
and start to fall from the sides, then rinse and drain them.

—Rinse and drain whenever they rattle a little or look or feel
dry.

—Keep the jar on its side. Protect the opening from drying
out too much.

—Keep the bottle in a dark place at room temperature for the
first four days. Expose them to the light for two or three
days, so the sprouts will develop little green leaves.

—Draining after each rinsing is done several ways. I hold a
tea strainer over the opening of the jar and shake the water
out. If you want to tilt the jar and drain about an hour after
each rinsing, use a nylon stocking to keep the seeds from
falling out or fit a disk of stainless steel hardware cloth
into the jar ring.

—Remove ungerminated seeds and hulls that cling to the
bottle by plulling them out with your fingers or washing

the sprouts in a pan of water and floating the hulls off the top. (I like to put them in clean bottles every day or two.)

—Air dry the sprouts before storing in the refrigerator. If they are not *too wet*, they will keep for weeks.

—*Note:* For variety, sprout different seeds together like alfalfa, radish, mustard and lettuce, or alfalfa and water cress seed.

Chapter 8

Extending Your Harvest Season

THERE IS A FRIENDLY COMPETITIVE SPIRIT among gardeners to see who has the first radishes, peas, corn or tomatoes of the season. I remember mother's envy as she once opened a letter from a sister-in-law living in a warmer climate. She had enclosed a tendril from her pea vines as proof of their earlier development.

Seedlings Grown Indoors

It is more convenient to buy tomato, pepper and other plants when it is the right time to set them out in the garden. But learning to grow them indoors saves money and prepares us for the time when they may not be available. Here's how:

—Use any container that will hold three or four inches of soil.
—Loose, light weight soil that will hold moisture is needed. Use two parts garden loam, one part sand and one part pulverized dry leaves (vermiculite or sphagnum moss may be used).
—Sterilizing the soil kills weed seeds and fungus parasites that attack tiny plants as they emerge from the soil. (However, some think this is unnecessary.) To sterilize, put soil in a roasting pan. Sprinkle it with a cup of water. Leave in oven 180° for one hour. Cool before planting.
—Plant seeds close together, thinning later with tweezers.
—Keep damp. (Water from underneath if the container has drainage.) It is the roots that need the water. Keeping the top of the soil a bit on the dry side discourages fungus growth.
—For good root growth, start seeds in a cool room about 50°.

—Transplant when the third leaves appear (true leaves).
—Space plants about an inch or so apart in flats, cold frames, pieces of milk cartons or in plant bands.
—Use a richer soil, putting less moss or sand in it.
—When the plant is about six inches high, begin to toughen the plant. (Any compassionate soul would understand that a fragile seedling grown in a protected environment should not be immediately thrust out under the rigors of full sun, storms, wind and rain.) Gradually expose the plants to more and more of the outside elements.
—Water the plants an hour or so before the final transplanting to the ground. Plant in the evening or on a cloudy day.

Creating More Heat for Early and Late Plants

—Bottles over plants give them an "individual greenhouse." A gardener in California had 200 narrow-necked gallon glass bottles (with the bottom "dish" cut off about two inches from the bottom). Peppers, tomatoes and other plants under bottles matured much earlier than those without a "greenhouse."
—Hotcaps, cold frames, plastic "tents" and watering with warm water, all help plants mature earlier.
—A high wood fence at the north end of the garden will reflect the sun and act as a wind break.
—Stake tomatoes against a south wall, if they need more heat.
—Rocks hold the heat and give warmth as they surround small plants. A two-foot wide stone mulch (flat surface up) prolonged the use of a garden for over a month. Plant early lettuce between the rocks with hot caps over them. You can do the same with late salad vegetables in the fall.

Follow the Sun — If you are determined to win the race of eating out of your garden first, you might try planting in a wheelbarrow and follow the sun with it. Or put your strawberry barrel on a plant dolly, with concealed casters, and do the same.

Early and Late Carrots; Other Hardy Plants

—To be the first to eat carrots out of your garden, plant seeds in pots indoors and transplant them outdoors when the weather warms up. Sow seeds about an inch apart in a pot or can of light soil. When seedlings are up, they may need thinning so they may grow evenly spaced. When they are a few inches high and the ground is warm, turn the clump of carrots out of the pot and plant in the ground. Allow about a foot square for each pot of carrots.

In the Northwest, I have planted carrots on September 15th and had finger-size carrots for Thanksgiving dinner.

I remember watching a "master gardener" reach down and wrap his big hand around the tops of a bunch of carrots, and with a quick yank he pulled them all up at once, cleaned them off with a squirt of the hose and handed me a bright orange "bouquet." I was determined to grow carrots the way he did.

It is easy to be discouraged when the seeds do not come up at all, or the carrots have a strong taste and pale color. They can be tough and fiberous with the tops breaking off when you pull them, or they can crack and split and be crooked and deformed. While visiting my brother in California, I was shown a demonstration on a guaranteed way to grow carrots. This I observed:

—The soil was very loose, light and fertile—no lumps.
—It was soaked for about four hours (the water table was low in the dry season of the year.)
—The seeds were soaked for about three days.
—They were air dried enough to handle, then mixed with sand (1/4 oz. seed in a cup of sand is enough for 100 foot row).
—Seeds were sprinkled in a shallow trench and covered with 1/2 inch or less of find loose compost or something similar.
—Now a flat board was used to firm the seeds to secure good contact between sand and soil and to remove air pockets.
—A wire mesh over the seed bed kept dogs and birds away.
—A gentle sprinkle of water over the top was the last "drink" they would get until they germinated about two weeks later. (In extreme heat, a burlap covering over the seeds sprinkled with water would keep the seeds moist without disturbing them.)

My last hurdle in growing perfect carrots was to stop planting them so thick. One year we thinned out 30 pounds of carrot tops from three 20 foot rows. Big straight carrots need to be 1½ to 2 inches apart in the rows, thinned when four inches high and again when they get crowded.

Carrots need consistent moisture to keep growing at a steady pace and be smooth and tender. If the soil around them is as tight as a corset, the carrots will grow bumpy (an old timer told me). A fiberglas root cellar would be convenient to store them in. A cool storage of about 35° and a humidity of about 90° is ideal.

Last March I was teaching a class on vitamins and minerals and took a basket of food that had survived the winter. I dug it from ground lightly covered with snow. Young mothers were surprised that I had hard crisp carrots, new cabbage leaves on a stalk, parsnips, rhubarb, comfrey and alfalfa just coming up, dandelion greens, a clump of chives, a cluster of garlic cloves, and a pan of Jerusalem artichokes.

Successive Planting

I do not want my garden vegetables to come and go all at once. In August of 1972 while driving home from Utah, we stopped at a farming community and found the harvest season all finished (at least at the home we visited). How depressing to see dry brown ground with nothing green in the garden. "What do they eat?" I thought.

Arriving home in the early morning, I took a basket and went straight to the garden—offering a silent prayer for a variety of food that was growing. I gathered:

green peppers	pan of potatoes
onions	gallon green peas
butter crunch lettuce	(edible pods)
cucumbers	string beans
radishes	zucchini
garden cress	kohlrabi
parsley	armful of chard
one ripe tomato	garbanzo (two in a
bunch of carrots	pod were forming)

Scarlet runner beans were in full bloom, strawberries from everbearing vines were still producing, as well as raspberries, blueberries and boysenberries. Roses, dahlias, carnations and petunias were blooming. I was surrounded with beauty and the bounties of this life.

Without successive plantings, many of the foods I gathered would have been past their peak and ready for the compost heap. Some of the late plantings are sometimes killed by frost before they mature, but it is worth the gamble of losing a few seeds and a little time.

Warding Off Frost

One family in Utah saved a favorite apricot tree in bud from a severe frost by the warmth from Christmas tree lights they hung on the branches. We are all familiar with commercial smudge pots to keep fruit from freezing, but I have seen home owners build fires under trees in small stoves or cans to create warmth.

To protect tomatoes and peppers from frost in the late fall, I draped a thin sheet of plastic over the rows and anchored it at the ends of the rows to pegs. I used clothespins to hold it on. We may not always have plastic, so I save burlap bags, old blankets and drapes to use for such purposes.

From experience I've learned other ways of warding off frost:

1. Spraying frosted plants with water before the sun comes up will often save them.

2. Allow a sprinkler to run on vegetables throughout frosty nights.

3. A dense foliage of radishes, turnips or other leafy vegetables planted close together helps ward off frost.

4. Vegetables close to the ground, with a wood chip mulch under them, will not freeze readily.

5. A heavy mulch of straw or hay over a strawberry bed or carrot rows will help.

6. Berry vines trailing on the ground should be left there until spring. (They are less likely to freeze than if up on wires.)

7. Snow is a good insulator. Relatives in Utah showed me kale, potatoes, carrots and other vegetables dug out of a snow bank. (Mustard sown as a cover crop will stand frost.)

8. Reports are that vegetables will not freeze as readily in humus-rich soil.

Storage Tips

Of course, it is more convenient to have vegetables stored in a fiberglass root cellar [1] near the kitchen door, than going out in cold stormy weather to get them out of the ground.

—Dry maple leaves make good insulating material for storing vegetables in bins.

---

1. Lynwil Industries, 3065 West 21st South, Salt Lake City, Utah 84119, telephone 801-487-3796, sells the root cellars. They are set in the ground with only a small lid and vents showing.

—Grapes packed in dry sawdust will keep for some time.

—Never store apples in the same pit with potatoes. The apples will taste odd.

(*Note:* See pages 112-114, *Passport to Survival*, for food storage ideas. Also in a new book, *Stocking Up*, by Rodale Press, are plans for constructing underground storage pits.)

Chapter 9

Growing Vegetables in a Drought

I HAVE ALWAYS ASSOCIATED DROUGHT with the death of living things, but learning about it has lifted that dismal feeling. The good Lord does send rain and snow, and He did intend during the dry seasons for the earth to hold (like a great basin) enough water for us all—man, plant and animal. We need to cooperate or His plan does not work.

We have to do more than build dams. We have to loosen our soil so the rains can penetrate instead of running off and flooding. We cannot continue to cover the face of the earth with concrete and expect the earth to absorb the rains from above.

I gardened in the Los Angeles area for ten years, under what seemed like drought conditions compared to the wet northwest. I have learned valuable agronomy lessons from these extreme climates and also from watching the struggle to keep things alive during a drought in Manila and during the dry season in Israel, Thailand and India. We now have laws that permit cloud seeding. It seems the right computations necessary to prevent tragedy haven't been perfected yet, according to the November 1977 issue of *Acres, U.S.A.* that reported on the September flood in Kansas City. You wonder if God intended for man to control the weather.

Preparing the Soil for Drought Conditions

Knowledge of soils is necessary if plants are to survive a drought. Later chapters will more completely cover soils and mulches. We need to make sure the soil in our garden is capable of holding the water it receives.

While observing two problem soils, I learned a lesson about the value of humus and moisture retention in a drought. Coarse sandy soil in Louisiana immediately soaked up buckets of water (as my daughter and I were transplanting some large plants). Without continuous watering, they would never survive. Fine clay soil, at my brother's home near San Francisco, desperately needed humus to loosen its cement-like qualities so moisture could penetrate. (The sandy soil needed humus to keep water from going through it so fast.)

In preparing these two soils for a drought, the procedure is the same: Add more humus, any mature vegetation, or animal manures. It is interesting that 100 pounds of humus holds 195 pounds of water like a sponge. Some soils will not hold thirty pounds of water.[1]

One thing we do have control over in our own garden spot is the fertility of the soil and its ability to absorb winter rains and snows. It gives a feeling of security to know our soil is prepared for its time of crisis.

Plant and Seed Selection

Plant early to beat the drought — Do not worry so much about a drought, just plant early and preserve the surplus.

Deep rooted perennials like asparagus, comfrey and alfalfa are sure to find enough moisture to mature. (I planted 100 more asparagus plants this spring.)

Plant an abundance of green leafy vegetables, a few weeks earlier than usual. You may have to replant, but it may be worth the gamble. Preserve the surplus; put a few bushels of green leaves in the freezer for green drinks or dry and powder them for soups and broth. If there is no drought, return unused amounts to the soil.

We can always eat the dry corn and beans from our food storage, if they don't mature in the garden, under drought conditions. In Missouri last summer, I walked the streets in an area where people had planted small gardens. In the late afternoons they sat on their porches viewing their wilted greens, dried up corn rows, parched lawns and dead flowers. Instead of looking glum and discouraged, I would go down to the river near by and bring up buckets of water, or else get the dead plants out of sight and be happy I had food storage to rely on.

1. Dr. Joe Nichols, Reprint No. 58, Lee Foundation for Nutritional Research.

Drought-resistant Seeds

—Buy seeds listed as drought resistant. Midget and dwarf varieties will ripen sooner.

—Some good dry climate plants are: New Zealand spinach, Chinese cabbage, collards (like cabbage), sunflowers, butternut squash and millet. (India is the world's leading grower of millet.)

—Seeds that fall to the ground from spinach and parsley, for example, will often winter over and come up again in the spring without much additional water.

Conserving Moisture

Ration the Water to a Few Plants

In a drought it is better to have a few vegetables survive than none at all. If plants are too crowded, they should be thinned. If crops have not been planted, the best solution is to plant them farther apart than usual. Plant cabbage four feet apart. Plant seeds in a row farther apart and down in a deep row to provide some shade.

Newspaper

Shredded newspaper soaked in water, a little lime, and high nitrogen fertilizer can be put in a hole about 12 inches deep and filled up with soil. A plant can be put in the center, and the newspaper will help keep the moisture down around the roots.

Plastic

Our main concern has been to keep the vegetables growing. Trees and other plants need water, too. If you live in an area where the humidity is very high, try this: tie a piece of 9 x 12 plastic over a limb of a tree like a dome. Fasten with masking tape. The water will collect in the plastic instead of evaporating in the air. Let it drip from the plastic into a basin dug around the tree. (Or let it drip into a bucket and water a shallow rooted plant.)

Mulch

Deep mulch around the plants will help hold the moisture down around the roots and prevent moisture from evaporating into the air. Don't wait until mid-July during a drought to look for mulch. (Collect great amounts of leaves or whatever is available in your area to shade the ground.

Shade

Shade the ground. Shade the plants.

1. Shade many fragile crops with a lath house.
2. Make a sun filter of screen wire on a simple frame to cover smaller plants.
3. Use a portable structure with burlap.
4. Use a leaning board to shade newly-planted rows.
5. Shade with cut saplings. (Plant some fast-growing trees for this purpose.)
6. Use a 6" wood shingle for partial shade for individual plants, pushing it into loose soil on the west side of each plant, so it gets the morning sun and not the hot afternoon sun.
7. Bigger leafed plants near smaller ones may provide needed shade. Bigger leaf soy beans can shade bush beans, or big leaves of the squash plant can shade lettuce.
8. Plant in a cold frame for shade.

Do's and Don'ts of Watering

Try using these tips to make your watering more efficient:
—Use a plastic soaker to conserve water.
—Water plants when they need it most—when they are first planted and when they are beginning to mature.
—To conserve water and get maximum growth, water plants when the soil micro-organism growth is the highest. In my area it is April, May, August and September.
—Planting a cover crop like rye in the fall slows down run-off of winter rains.
—Overhead watering is a waste of water, and so is running water from a hose on the surface of the soil and watering in the heat of the day. The loss from evaporation is great.
—Water plants individually. Put a leaking can in the ground by each one, a gallon can (or smaller) of water in which a small nail hole has been punched. This allows the water to leak out very slowly near the plant roots where it will do the most good. The drip method of watering is used in Israel and other places to conserve water. Water from plastic pipe drips on each plant along the rows.

—In El Salvador children in the family carried well water in plastic bowls and poured it into furrows; then they helped to plant the seeds.
—Catch rain water in a barrel for the garden.
—Maybe you have wet spots in the garden. Use a dry well (a hole full of stone or gravel) to drain them. Placement of watering ditches for downward flow is important.

Don't Worry—Plant and Prepare

In a hotel in India, the water from the wash basins drained out through a hole near the floor to water a row of flowers below. In Thailand, ornate water jugs were lined up on the walks leading to the homes, and the lids were removed when it rained. In my youth cisterns were common as receptacles to catch and hold valuable rain water.

The juice in melons was the only liquid a group of bushmen in Southern Africa had to save their lives and that of their animals.[1] We should remember this and use the water in oversized cucumbers, summer squash and imperfect melons to water other plants.

It is interesting that nature gave moth caterpillars the instinct to eat the leaves off a big tree during a drought to save the tree. (The leaves grow back again.)

Pray for rain. Ezra Taft Benson, after visiting the South West area of the United States during a serious drought, called for a day of prayer for rain on April 26, 1955. Latter-day Saint (Mormon) President Spencer W. Kimball also called for a week of prayer and fasting in February of 1977 to alleviate drought conditions.

The Navajo Indian rain dances imploring to Deity for rain showed their great faith.

---

1. National Geographic Society Television program, "Bushmen of the Kalahari." Mr. Marshall visited these people. (His sister wrote a best seller book about them—I can't locate it.)

Chapter 10

Unusual Plants and Planting Ideas

Food Crops Seldom Grown at Home

SOME PLANTS MENTIONED HERE may be common in your garden, but most people buy them in the market with never a thought of growing them at home.

Peanuts — Peanuts and sweet potatoes were two favorite crops in our Victory Garden years ago in Burbank, California.

1. About four shelled red Spanish raw peanuts were planted in each hill and covered with two inches or less of soil. The hills were 18 inches apart in rows two feet apart.

2. We added compost to our rather sandy soil.

3. Leaves appeared in about two weeks. When about a foot high, we banked the soil, so it almost touched the lower leaves. The soil has to be within easy reach and loose enough so the flower stem can turn and go down into the soil. It forms the seed (peanut) from the flower right there in the soil.

4. The leaves are small, fluttery and pretty. When they turn yellow in the fall, it is time to lift out the plant with a fork, pick off the peanuts and dry in a hot garage. In colder climates they should be left in the ground probably until the first frost darkens the leaves.

Sweet Potatoes — To grow your own starts, put a few sweet potatoes in a shallow pan of water. After about a month, when the plants (that grow out of the potato) are about four inches high, they are ready to plant in the garden. Cut so there is a plant on each piece of potato. Plant in rows about a foot apart and hill up around each plant as it grows. Dig potatoes after the first frost. Before storing, dry off and harden the skin for about two weeks at approximately 80°. Store in temperatures above 50°.

It is a slow process for a plant to "put together" a big, heavy, solid, sweet tuber. In California it took four or five months. The tubers in the rainy Northwest are smaller and not as sweet. But, the leaves are beautiful and I just learned they are good to eat.[1]

Mushrooms — Growing mushrooms indoors requires a cold dark place with a temperature under 65°. If there is an energy crisis, maybe we can have mushrooms growing in dark corners of the house and then use them to make gourmet dishes with our wheat and grains.

They are a rapidly-growing fungus, but I think of them as an ordinary plant because I can go to the seed store and buy spawn by the pound. It keeps like seeds and you don't have to use it all up at once. It takes about five weeks for mushrooms to grow. They yield four or five crops a year from one planting.

Amaranth Grain — See proteins, Part III. If you want to experiment growing this decorative, high protein food plant, contact the Amaranth Information Bureau, Rodale Press, Inc., 33 East Minor Street, Emmaus, Pennsylvania 18049.

Watercress — This can be grown from seed, but it is easier to buy a bunch at the market and put a few stems in a pot of wet sand to root. (They will root in water if you change it every day.) When the cress has good heavy roots, transplant in separate pots and keep the pots in water at all times. This may be done either in a tray of water in a north window or outside in a child's plastic wading pool sunk in the ground. Try to duplicate its native habitat—cool, clean water in a cool place with partial shade. Ideal soil to plant in is sifted humus from the woods mixed with garden soil and a little ground limestone.

Chayote — This is an old food crop making a comeback. It is an unusual squash, rich in iron. While it takes a hot climate to flower and fruit, its roots and leaves are nourishing, tasty and edible. As a vine, it is useful for shade and grows very fast.

Chia Seed — If I lived in the desert, I would plant Chia seeds. It is a high energy food and presently very expensive.

Jicama — (Pronounced "Hi-Kah-Mah.") This has the texture of a crisp juicy apple. It resembles an oversized turnip in appearance. It grows in swamps and is a staple food in Mexico. Friends vacationing there have promised to bring back seeds to plant. It is a favorite raw vegetable.

---

1. Bargyla and Gylver Rateaver, "The Organic Method Primer," Pauma Valley, California, published by authors, 1973, page 153.

Chlorella — This is a fast growing algae. Algae grow both in sea water and fresh water. In Thailand I visited an orchard where the water in deep ditches between the rows was covered with the green algae and was being skimmed off. It can be used to feed plants, animals and man. In powder form, it can be used in breads and other foods. It can be purchased as a high protein food supplement. As food for mankind gets scarce, we may hear more of this food.

Gardening Ideas, Old and New

Electro Culture — Anything metal in the garden is said to increase the electricity in the atmosphere. This increases the cellular activity in plants, resulting in better growth. In one California garden, I saw strange things: wires over the rows fastened to metal stakes at both ends, tin cans around the pepper plants and tin lids dangling from tomato plants. (A laser beam is now being used to speed up plant growth.)

Pyramid Planting — The old but new concept is that an apparatus pointing north over the planting area (a framework or greenhouse) stimulates the growth of plants, and helps preserve them.

Two-Level Planting and Space Saving Ideas — Keep up the fertility of the soil in close planting when roots are competing for food. Put a tomato plant down through a hole in a big potato and have tomatoes bear on top of the ground and potatoes underneath. This works—I tried it.

Put a tire around a potato plant. As it grows, fill inside the tire with soil. Repeat until you have four tires on top of each other. A Montana housewife succeeded in harvesting almost 100 pounds of potatoes from one plant.

Plant peanuts and squash in the same row, occupying space above and below.

Plant early crops like radishes or lettuce with a late bell pepper crop. Transplant to get another crop growing faster. Replant "thinnings" from beets, kohlrabi, lettuce and chard. Peas, carrots and beans can also be transplanted, but the yield may decrease.

Let beans climb the corn stalks.

Plant pumpkins in the corn rows (to stumble over).

Planting in Rugged Ground — Squash, cucumbers, potatoes, pumpkins and melons can be planted on rugged ground in weeds and grass. (How successful the crops are, however, will depend on rainfall and fertility of the soil.) The plants can be fertilized with foliage spray. First loosen the soil where you are going to plant. Flatten the weeds and grass and cover with hay. The vines will develop their fruit on the surface of the hay. (Plant asparagus seed in the weeds along a ditch bank.)

Save Splitting Cabbage — If cabbage is splitting from too much rain, straddle it and yank it gently. This will break off some of the fine roots so less water is taken from the ground to the cabbage, which causes it to swell and burst.

Have a Plan — My current choice of a garden plan is the mound system used in China—raised beds of soil with sloping sides and narrow walkways in between. You can cultivate and harvest without stepping on the beds. The dimensions are 25 feet long, 4 feet wide at the bottom (3 feet wide at top), 6 inches high with 18-inch paths. (Boards on the sides of raised beds provide too comfortable a place for slugs and bugs to hide and live in comfort.)

If I were starting a garden in a new location, I would consider the following:

1. A small garden near the kitchen door. I like to hurry out and pick a sprig of parsley, herbs for seasoning, salad vegetables or comfrey for a green drink.

2. Plan designated areas for (a) perennials like asparagus, comfrey, alfalfa, Jerusalem artichokes; (b) establish a place for a child's jungle garden where anything that feels like growing can be assured a home. An assortment of left-over seeds could be used. (c) Have a seed-saving area where a carrot, radish, or parsnip could be left alone to go to seed. (I don't like to see a big straggly plant going to seed where new ones are coming in.) (d) Provide for garden equipment needs—they need an inconspicuous spot to call home.

Roots — Do not plant gardens near shallow-rooted trees like elm, maple, poplar or willow.

Saving Seeds

Saving seeds from our own vegetables is almost a lost art. Seeds to plant may be a necessity of life. Along with the vacuum packed seeds on my storage shelf are others I have learned to save.

Kinds of Seeds to Save — Begin with non-hybrid annual plants like peas, beans, peppers, tomatoes, lettuce, spinach, radishes, onions, cucumbers and potatoes. To get seeds from carrots, parsley and celery, you have to wait until the second year.

Peas — (a) Watch for the first formed pods. (b) Tie colored yarn on the vines so you will not pick them. (c) Let pods ripen completely. (d) Pull the vines and hang them under a shelter until pods are brittle. (e) Shell the peas and store. (See "Seed Saving Ideas," at the bottom of this page.)

Tomatoes — (a) Choose "seed carriers" from vines with vigorous growth and good color. (b) Mark the vines. (c) Leave the tomatoes on the vine until they are overripe, but not spoiled. (d) Cut the tomato and remove the seeds with some of the pulp. (e) Soak them about two days in water until they start to ferment, but do not sprout. (f) Rub the pulp off the seed and spread them thinly on paper. (g) Dry them rapidly, but not in direct sunlight.

Carrots — (a) Either leave the carrots you have selected for seed in the ground all winter with a heavy mulch on top and let them start growing again in the spring, or (b) dig up the carrots and keep them in damp sand and then plant them in the ground again the following spring. Seeds form the second year. (c) When the seeds are formed and dry, shake them into a paper bag. When almost ripe, tie a paper bag over the tops to keep seeds from falling to the ground.

Onions — In Utah one fall, after long warm summer days, a row of multiplier onions opened up their "pom poms" to reveal hundreds of tiny black seeds. With delight, I shook them in a sack and planted the next spring. I broadcast them very thickly. They came up like wheat grass. I transplanted them in rows and had plenty of green onions.

Grow your own onion sets for the next spring by planting about a quarter ounce of seed in a space about two-foot square. The plants have to grow in crowded conditions, so they will not get any bigger than the end of your thumb. Most of the tops will fall over when they are ripe. Pull and cut off all but a short piece of the top. Store in net bags.

Seed Saving Ideas — Year after year my neighbor plants a big garden with seeds she has saved herself.

—She makes sure the seeds are dry so they will not mold.
—She never treats any of her seeds.
—The seeds are stored in small bottles on a garage shelf.
—She labels and dates them with a water-proof marking pen.
—Few seeds, she says, will germinate as soon as they ripen.
 A rest period from a month to a year is required (except for

wheat that sprouts in the seed head, if it is wet at harvest time).

—To determine what percent of your seeds will grow, count out about twenty seeds and see how many will sprout. Soak the seeds (in milk to speed up germination), drain and spread between a moist cloth on a dish. Keep damp. It may take two days or two weeks to germinate.

—Good germination can be expected from corn and onions stored for two years; beans, peas and parsley, three years; tomatoes, four years; cabbage and spinach, five years; beets and squash, six years.

Chapter 11

How to be a Plant Doctor

Preventive Care Begins with the Soil

EVERY GROWING SEASON, I learn more about what makes plants sick or well. These are my strong convictions:
- —The health of the soil influences the health of plants (and every other living thing).
- —Healthy plants build up an immunity to harmful insects.
- —Deficiency symptoms and hunger signs in plants can be recognized with training.
- —Plants strive to help themselves and will join forces with other plants and living things (if given a chance) in prevention and cure of plant disease.

My husband has been doctoring our sick, worn out soil for a long time. Its recovery is encouraging, but now the noisy shredder is silenced after cutting up tons of leaves, limbs, corn stalks, garbage and manure to feed the soil. When I'm as old as Ruth Stout, author of *The No Work Garden Book,* we won't need any more power equipment—just hay for mulch, a pitchfork to lift it with, a few seeds, and then I can rest on the couch most of the day.

Emergency Measures for Insect Control

In order to keep the bugs from eating all our crops (while we are concentrating on improving our soil), we may need:

Rotenone for such pests as cabbage worm, sowbugs (pillbugs), earwigs, wireworms, spittle bugs, caterpillers and other insects. Rotenone is the powdered root of a tropical plant and is also found in a native weed called Devil's Shoestring. It is considered harmless to man and animal. (Note: Do not breathe or use on food crops the day they are harvested. Rotenone loses toxicity in storage in about one year. [1]

Pyrethrum, known as painted daisy (a perennial plant). The powdered petals of the daisy make a good botanical insecticide, but it is not widely sold today. I would like to grow the flowers, mix with some Fullers earth and use it as a dust or spray.

Nicotine sulphate (sold as Black Leaf 40), acts as a stomach poison to insects. It is highly toxic to humans if taken internally. It is used on many small insects like those that take bites out of peas and beans. Nicotine sulphate is hard to find. Cigarette ends can be collected and used to make a spray. Boil one pound of cigarette ends in two gallons of water for 30 minutes. Strain through a piece of nylon. It will keep several weeks in a sealed jar. (Use one-half pound if you have non-filter tip cigarettes.) Dilute with four parts of water to one of nicotine for a spray for anything hard to kill. Water with it along the rows. For cabbage moth caterpillars, mix a quart of the solution with one ounce of soft soap and spray on plants. Do not forget that this is a poison and highly toxic to humans if taken internally; so label all containers of the nicotine. Do not eat anything that has been sprayed with it for two weeks.

Sabadilla dust,[2] made from seeds of a Venzuelan plant, is toxic to insects only and is for things hard to kill, such as beetles and grasshoppers. It stores well.

Basic-H [3] is made of three vegetable oils. Two teaspoons or less in a gallon of water, sprayed on soft-bodied pests, will penetrate the waxy coating on their bodies and dehydrate them.

Diatomaceous earth, a mined product used as a dust, smothers insects. (It also absorbs moisture in dried food, prevents mildew, rust and fungus in damp climates.)

Dusts and Sprays Made from Plants

If we didn't have access to any of the products mentioned, we could discourage bugs by using strong smelling and tasting plants in various ways. We often have a surplus of:

1. Rateaver, Bargyla and Gylver, "Organic Method Primer," California, 1973. Published by the authors, Pauma Valley, California 92061. Read Chapter 13, page 180.
2. Ibid.
3. Ibid.

Marigolds (I have a gallon of   Horseradish
  powdered petals)   Garlic
Nasturtiums   Onions
Dandelions   Yarrow
Sunflower leaves   Tansy
Rhubarb   Russian Nap weed
Tomato vines   Basil, sage and other
Elderberry leaves   culinary herbs

These plants could be:
—Dried and powdered for a dust.
—Picked fresh, put in a blender with water and used as a
  spray.
—Chopped and worked into the soil.
—Planted near certain plants.
—Or branches could be placed around plants you are pro-
  tecting.
A combination of these methods should make the environment unbearable for insects.

Household Supplies to Control Insects

Supplies that are ready to be thrown out can often be salvaged and used in the war against insects.

Dry milk powder   Cayenne pepper
Rancid oil or grease   Old soap scraps
Strong molasses   Sour milk
Mustard powder   Salt
White flour or sugar

For additional information on homemade pesticides, read *In Place of Poisons,* Henry Doubleday Research Association, 20 Convent Lane, Bocking, Braintree, Essex, England.

Biological Control

My parents in the country didn't worry much about a pest control program, and their soil was not as worn out as most of ours is today. They had bantam hens running about picking up bugs and worms and eating off the weeds. Turkeys, ducks and geese[1] did the same. Plentiful too were birds, bats, lizards,

----

1. Families near me with fenced-in gardens have geese that gulp down the slugs but don't eat the vegetables.

toads, snakes, hawks, owls and seagulls who ate off the land. Lady bugs were everywhere; so were ant hills, moths, spiders, dragon flies, bees, wasps and yellow jackets (that ate the cabbage worms).

Now most of us live in the city, and we don't want grey wasps nests hanging in the corner of the porch or big spider webs or chickens running loose. Some gardeners are buying lady bugs to release over the garden—or praying mantis, lacewing fly and trichogramma wasp to eat the insects.

Trees and hedges around our homes are natural habitats of birds. Some birds eat their own weight in insects every day. They also eat weed seeds. I watched a bird land on the side of a tall stem, bend it to the ground with its weight, walk out to the end, and proceed to eat the weed seeds.

Know Your Pests

Gardeners I know who really have productive crops have a vast knowledge of insect life. They know what their "enemy" looks like. (See pictures in *Sunset Basic Gardening Illustrated*, $1.95.) They observe their actions—even at night with a flashlight. They know other things, such as:
—Where insects lay their eggs so they can destroy their nests at the right time.
—How they survive from season to season and what conditions foster or hinder their growth.

Lures and Traps for Pillbugs and Earwigs — I am amused at the strategy gardeners use to lure pests away from food crops. A subtle trick I observed in California to keep pillbugs (or sow bugs) off the crops was to provide them with fresh leaves (for food and shelter) down the middle of the rows. As I lifted up the leaves, the bugs rolled into pills and formed a black band of squirming, moving bugs, content to eat, live, reproduce and die in the same spot, which added fertility to the soil. The following spring vegetable seeds were planted where the bugs had been while they fertilized another strip.

Aphid Control
—Squirt them off the plants with a stream of water.
—Put on a glove and wipe them off the plant.
—Controlling ants decreases the aphids. Ants carry aphids around (tend them). They go up trees and even crawl on healthy plants.
—Cayenne pepper in solution is reported to kill aphids.

—Try a powder of sulphur and ashes.

—Rhubarb leaves (or elder leaves). Cut up three pounds of rhubarb leaves, boil for half an hour in three quarts of water and strain. When cool, dissolve one ounce of soap-flakes in a quart of water. Mix the two and use as a general spray for any aphids.

—My pole beans were black with aphids. Why? It was raining when I picked the beans, which encouraged aphids and bacteria to spread. (Bacteria must have moisture to multiply.) The rows were crowded close together, which prevented good air circulation, and the soil was poor.

Cabbage Family Problems

—A neighbor has no trouble with maggots on the cabbage roots when she slips a four inch square of building paper (slit to the center) soaked in creosote around the base of the plant. It is held in place by covering over with a little soil.

—Look for the eggs that resemble grains of rice on the surface of the ground and remove by hand. If they are already working on the stem and the plant looks wilted, pull back the dirt and mix about five teaspoons wood ashes with some soil around the plant. Firm it down and water well.

Other Cabbage Insects — The larvae of the white butterfly look like small green worms. The eggs are laid at the base of the leaf and are hard to see. Either cover the cabbage plants with cheesecloth or net so the butterfly or moth cannot lay its eggs on the leaves, or remove the eggs with a wet tissue. Wash the leaves and sprinkle with ashes, or Rotenone dust can be used.

Bigger Pests: Slugs, Snails, Moles, Gophers, Rats and Mice

Slugs — In my wet country slugs are a problem. They need to keep their skins moist in order to survive and slide along. Grit and dry ground are painful to their soft bodies. To prevent them from chewing on plant leaves or on the roots of perennial plants in the winter, remove a little soil around each plant and put a barrier of:

coarse sand	straw (chopped)
ashes	nut shells or any
crushed egg shells	sharp material
dry chaff	

During the day slugs hide in any cool dark place they can find. At night and early in the morning they come out to feed on tender leaves.

We found cans to be a good slug trap. Use any can with a plastic lid. Cut two or three rectangular windows in the sides of the can about an inch from the closed bottom of the can. Put the can down into the ground to the bottom of the little window. Put commercial slug bait in the bottom of the can (or use yeast dissolved in water or jelly and water or beer). The plastic lid on the can keeps the rain from diluting the bait and keeps dogs, cats and birds from getting into it. Add the dead slugs to the compost pile and use the bait again. Paint the cans all a uniform pretty color.

Moles and Gophers — I do not remember mole or gopher mounds in the lawn or garden in the country. Dad said the owls, hawks, snakes and coyotes captured them for food. Since we do not have many of these around in the cities, we need to find other means of control.

—They make a vast underground network of runways which they use to find food. They literally swim through the ground if it is loose and fertile.

—They lift up plants and eat earthworms.

—They carry bacteria from one diseased plant to another.

—Mice, rats and gophers use mole runways and do as much damage as the moles.

Traps seem to be the best control for rodents. Cats can be trained to hunt gophers. They may bring in several a day if you praise them enough when they do it.

Send for illustrated circulars on *Mole and Gopher Control,* No. 534, California Agricultural Experiment Station, Extension Service, University of California.

Rats and members of the rodent family can be driven out of an area with an ultrasonic frequency that will cause rats and rodents to go into a frenzy while trying to get away from it. It can be used to drive them away or flush them into the open where they can be killed. For more information write to: Scientific Systems, P. O. Box 716, Amherst, N. H. 03031.

Part III

More About the Best Foods

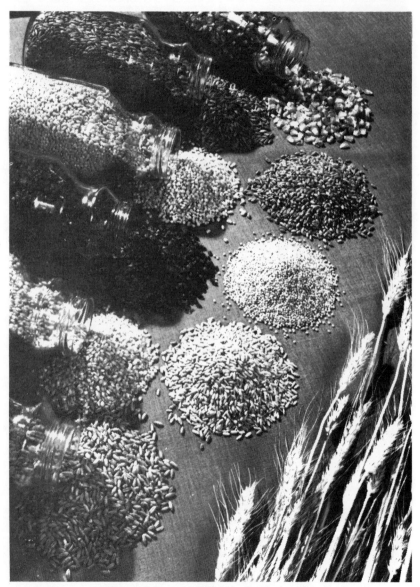

All grains are good for the food of man.

Chapter 12

Choosing and Preparing the Best Foods

Grains, Garden Vegetables, and Fruit

SURVIVAL IS THE MAIN CONCERN in this chapter about choosing the best foods. Circumstances and body needs will continue to vary for each of us. Perhaps you cannot plant a garden *today* or pick fruit from the trees you planted, but most people in this country could find some wheat to buy. Wheat and other grains are some of the best buys available. Properly stored they will keep beyond the year 2000. Grains have been the staff of life down through the ages because of their great nutritional value and storage qualities. Wheat will some day be a precious commodity. Although we do not rely heavily on it in meal planning today, our consumption of wheat could skyrocket during a prolonged food shortage, if it were available.

One solution to the world's food problems seems to be for individual families to plant gardens, fruit trees and store grains and other food. One author says protein is the "bull's eye" of food storage.

About Proteins

Meat for a Treat—in Winter Cold or Famine

Eating meat sparingly is a way of life for myself and many others. In an acute food shortage, we would be thankful for the continued use of small amounts of meat to season our vegetables and grains. Hopefully it will be fresh meat, maybe from our own rabbits or chickens. Canned or commercially-dehydrated animal proteins are being stored by many people.

Other Proteins and Fats — With or without meat we could use and store:
- —More grains,[1] potatoes, milk and cheese.
- —Soy beans and other dry beans and peas.[2]
- —Almonds, pecans, coconut, other nuts.
- —Protein powder.

Legumes in an array of colors, sizes and shapes. Left to right, front row: mung, chili beans, soy, black, Alaska peas, navy bean; back row: lupins, cranberry, garbanzos, scarlet runner, lima.

Proteins, fats and oils are also found in:
- —Fish, wheat germ, rice and corn.
- —Seeds: sunflower, sesame, pumpkin and flax.
- —Green and dried leaves, such as comfrey and alfalfa.
- —Oil in special sealed capsules is said to keep 20 years in a cool place.

The spotlight has been on protein in recent years. If it were in short supply and were rationed among various family members, the following should be considered:

---

1. Rodale Press, Inc., is conducting a research project on amaranth grain plant. It is higher in protein than wheat and corn. A friend gave me a large red and a green flowering head. (They were beautiful drying on a white sheet in an upstairs bedroom.) The grain from the heads rattling in my paper bag look almost as small as salt.

2. An array of colors, sizes and shapes of legumes adds pleasure to our job in the kitchen. See photo.

A common misconception is that we need protein for energy.[1] This is not true. Protein is strictly for cellular repair and replacement. Growing children, teen-agers, pregnant or nursing mothers, or an injured person would require as much or more protein than the father, even though he was doing hard physical work. He could use more carbohydrate for energy, while the others need the protein for building and repairing body tissue. In a day the father might get only 34 grams of protein from a cup of beans, a potato, a glass of milk and four slices of bread.

Hopefully, we will have fats and oils in our menus in some form, so we do not have dry skin outside and leathery cell walls (or membranes) inside. These tough walls make it difficult for body cells to receive nutrients and discharge wastes.

Better Protein Balance

Information on how to combine plant proteins for essential amino acid balance is available. What is lacking in most families (including mine) is the motivation to research the need for complete proteins and use different foods. It is easier to buy meat or disregard the subject.

I try to plan menus combining grains and legumes and grains and milk in various ways. We need less protein if it is in the form the body can use, combined right and prepared right. (See Chapter 13 on recipes.)

This analogy helped me to understand essential amino acids. If we had enough parts to build a dozen wheelbarrows and only one wheel, we could build only one workable wheelbarrow. The rest of the parts would be junked. If incomplete proteins are eaten, the body cannot use them for the purpose they were intended.

Too much protein may not be a problem in the future as it often is today. It contributes to kidney and heart disorders and the body's inability to retain calcium.

Note to Table 1 on following page: If animal proteins were not available (or we wanted to eat less), it is good to know that five ounces of dark leafy greens provide about five to six grams of protein. Soybean milk is found to be about 80% as potent as cow's milk in regard to its Vitamin B-complex content. The utilization of the calcium of soybean milk prepared in the traditional manner is about 90% that of cow's milk.

---

1. Dr. Sheldon C. Deal, "New Life Through Nutrition," New Life Publishing, 1974, 1001 North Swan Road, Tucson, Arizona 85711, page 24.

TABLE NO. 1

Protein yield of some common foods [1]

Protein 20-25 gm per serving (or nearly ½ the adult daily allowance)

		Cooked At. Gm.
Soy beans	1 cup	260
Other dry beans, peas	1½ cup	400
Meat, fish, poultry	3-3½ oz.	90-100

Protein 5-8 gm per serving

Milk	1 glass	200-400
Egg	1	50
Peanut butter	2 Tbsp	30
Bean or pea soup	3/4 cup	185

Protein 2-4 gm per serving

Bread	1 slice	25
Dark green vegetables	1/2-2/3 cup	70-120
Potato-white or sweet	1 medium	100

By combining wheat and beans (or other grains and legumes), for example, we get much higher percent of usable protein.

TABLE NO. 2: SUMMARY OF COMPLEMENTARILY [Protein] [2]

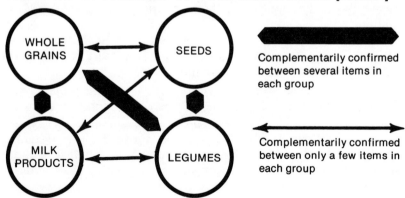

Complementarily confirmed between several items in each group

Complementarily confirmed between only a few items in each group

1. "BBC Nutrition and Physical Fitness," page 97.
2. "Diet for a Small Planet," page 124.

Value of Good Food Selection

It is my belief that proper food not only builds the mind and body, but influences the spirit and character as well. Now and in the days ahead, I need all the physical and spiritual strength possible. I need protection from disease, as far as possible, so I can look after my own needs and help my family and others as well.

As mentioned, it is possible for most people to select nutritionally-adequate diets from available food if the necessary information and motivation is provided. This is contingent, of course, on whether the food they like is available in adequate amounts at a price they can afford. There is no guarantee of this in the future.

We need to develop the ability to change our food habits and diet patterns. A lieutenant colonel in the Army lived mostly on hamburgers and salads, but was able to change his dietary habits. This is not easy, because many food likes and dislikes are set by three years of age. Physiological and emotional factors are closely tied with food habits and need to be understood.

When I was a youngster, our family of 11 surrounded the table together almost every morning, noon and night with not much to snack on inbetween. Times have changed today; many meals and snacks are eaten away from home. It seems the responsibility for adequate diet needs to be accepted and understood by each individual family member.

More Raw Vegetables

For the past two years, I have watched hungry Cub Scouts crunch on carrots, celery, turnips and alfalfa sprouts. I am sure they would also accept cauliflower, cabbage, wafer thin slices of raw potato, or zucchini for their refreshments occasionally. Yet research shows vegetables are among the foods least liked by teen-agers and young adults. All things which come of the earth in the season thereof were intended to please the eye and gladden the heart. This will happen as fresh food appears on the table with improved flavor, color and texture.
  —Raw foods increase the breathing of our cells and their oxygen utilization. (It is interesting to read about the light and spirit in plants.)
  —Eating raw foods is said to offset the bad effects of air pollution, and helps remove toxins from the body.

—They improve digestion, high vitality, and resistance to
disease.

Several changes my husband and I are making in food selection have contributed to a desired weight loss and more vibrant
health.

1. **Green drinks** — In cold weather this winter, I gathered
kale, turnip tops, collards, chickweed and other edible weeds and
plants. I would blend, strain and drink them, sometimes adding
pineapple or apple juice. If I could not get these plants, I would
grow wheat grass and buckwheat indoors. We continue through
the years to drink carrot juice and all the fresh fruit and vegetables
we can get. See chart on nutritive values of foods. Vitamin A and
C in fresh yellow and green food is not found in wheat. In the
future, we may be consuming more wheat, and the habit of drinking green drinks will be an advantage. Natural food supplements
are a part of many people's food storage.

2. **More roughage** — We need to eat more whole foods with
seeds, strings and skin intact. (I served my nine-year-old grand-
son homemade tomato soup with slivers of skin. He examined
and rejected it.) If I couldn't get an abundance of fresh fruit and
vegetables, we could eat bran every day for roughage.

3. **Less meat, dairy products, and desserts** — and more
nuts, soy beans and dried fruits.

4. **More water** — I'm finally convinced of the value. Women
report to me that water is an aid to beautiful skin.

5. **Variety of grains** — Corn, millet, buckwheat, rye, legumes, barley, tritacale, oats, rice, soy beans, lentils, and garbanzos. These all have varied nutrients the body needs.

—Millet has an alkaline reaction in the body and is higher in
  calcium, iron and vitamin B17 than wheat.
—Buckwheat contains a high grade protein and rutin that
  strengthens arterial walls. It contains B17 (for cancer
  control).
—Rye has more potassium than wheat.
—Barley we are told is for milk drinks. (Malt is made from
  about three-inch barley sprouts that are dried, ground and
  sifted.) It is higher in fat than wheat.
—Corn, oats and rice are all good grains to store. A new
  type of corn, called Opague-2, has nearly doubled the
  effective protein content of normal corn. It approaches
  that of meat, and surpasses that of milk. (*Readers Digest,*
  January, 1975, page 144.)

—Tritacale, a cross between wheat and rye, provides the best balance of the essential amino-acids of any grain.

I have learned how to combine and use grains and legumes, but the habit is not well established yet. Also, if fresh food were scarce, more of these foods would be used.

6. **Herbs** — We are depending more on herbs, learning of their value in prevention and cure of common disorders.

7. **Improved attitudes** contribute to well-being like improved food selection and preparation. We are working on this.

Reduced Losses of Nutrients in Food Storage, Handling and Preparation

Forming habits now in preparing food so it retains maximum nutrients will be valuable when food is more scarce.

1. **Whole grains** — No matter what kind of grain we are using, there is a loss in nutrients if the germ and bran have been removed in milling. For example, there is a 77 to 80 per cent loss of thiamin, riboflavin and niacin when using white flour. (See chart on "Losses of Nutrients in the Refining of Wheats," p. 126.)

2. **Fruits and vegetables** — Leafy green and yellow vegetables suffer the greatest loss of Vitamin C and certain B vitamins in cooking. (See chart on "Approximate Loss of Nutrients During Preparation and Cooking of Foods," p. 125.)

3. **Heat and protein** — Dr. Melchior Dikkers says this: Low heat, waterless cooking saves flavor, color, vitamins and minerals. It does not change the chemical nature of the proteins. Heat of cooking coagulates the meat proteins which actually thus become less readily digested by the protein-splitting enzymes in the digestive tract. Others state that cooking destroys part of many amino acids, thus distracting the amino-acid pattern and making most cooked proteins incomplete. [1] (I think of raw fish I ate in Denmark and of the other proteins that could be eaten uncooked: eggs, milk, nuts, seeds, some cheese.)

4. **Reheating foods** — holding for long periods—cooking water. I am learning to cook smaller amounts of food so it does not need reheating for another meal. But it is hard after cooking for a big family.

_____

1. Allan K. Smith, Ph.D., and Sidney J. Circle, Ph.D., "Soy Beans: Chemistry and Technology," Vol. 1, Westport, Connecticut, The AVI Publishing Company, Inc., 1972, pp. 226-229, 232.

TABLE NO. 3
Nutritive Values of Foods
in Average Servings or Common Measures [1]

Food	Weight gm	Approx. Measure	Calcium mg	Vit. A	Thiamin mg	Ribo-flavin mg	Niacin mg	Protein gm
Turnip greens boiled, drained	75	1/2 cup	138	4730	0.11	0.18	0.5	2.0
Beet greens boiled, drained	100	1/2 cup	99	5100	0.07	0.15	0.3	1.5
Beets cooked or canned, drained	85	1/2 cup	12	20	0.03	0.03	0.3	1.0
Dandelion greens boiled, drained	100	1/2 cup	140	11700	0.13	0.16	--	2.0
Kale leaves boiled, drained	55	1/2 cup	103	4570	0.06	0.10	0.9	2.5
Mustard greens boiled, drained	100	2/3 cup	138	5800	0.08	0.14	0.6	2.0
Parsley, raw chopped	3.5	1 Tbsp.	7	300	tr.	0.01	tr.	0.1
Carrots, raw grated	50	1/2 cup	19	5500	0.03	0.03	0.3	0.6
boiled, drained, diced	100	2/3 cup	33	10500	0.05	0.05	0.5	0.9
Chard, Swiss boiled	100	1/2 cup	3	5400	0.04	0.11	0.4	2.0
Wheat flour whole grain, stirred	120	1 cup	49	0	0.66	0.14	5.2	16.0

1. Boggert, Briggs, Calloway, "Nutrition and Physical Fitness," W. B. Saunders Co., 1973, 9th edition, West Washington Square, Philadelphia, Pennsylvania 19105.

Most food service operations hold food in warm places for long periods of time. Discarding even a tablespoon of water that vegetables are cooked in is a loss of nutrients.

These practices (and others, too) reduce the nutritional value of food.

During this "11th hour," we will find peace if we store what food we can, plant gardens if possible, use a variety of foods in the most efficient way, and experiment with simplified recipes.

TABLE NO. 4

Approximate Loss of Nutrients During Preparation and Cooking of Foods
(Percent Loss from Raw Product) [1]

	Thiamin	Riboflavin	Niacin	Vitamin C
Leafy green and yellow vegetables	45	40	40	50
Potatoes and sweet potatoes	25	20	20	35
Other vegetables and fruits	20	20	20	25
Citrus fruit and tomatoes	--	--	--	15

Food to Prepare at Home—A Blessing

Personal food reserves to prepare at home and fall back on would be a blessing if suddenly:
—There were no convenience foods on the market shelves.
—No eggs, meat, milk, citrus fruit or produce.
—Restaurants and hamburger stands closed up.
—There were no school lunch programs.
—There were no relief agencies, nursing homes, or senior citizen centers.

---

1. Bogert, Briggs, Calloway, "Nutrition and Physical Fitness," W.B. Saunders Co., 1973, West Washington Square, Philadelphia, Pennsylvania, 19105, 9th edition.

TABLE NO. 5

Losses of Nutrients on the Refining of Wheat [1]

Nutrient	Wheat pg gm	White Flour pg gm	Loss in White Flour, %
Percent of wheat	100	72	28.0
Thiamin	3.5	0.8	77.1
Riboflavin	1.5	0.3	80.0
Niacin	50	9.5	80.9
Vitamin B1	1.7	0.5	71.8
Pantothenic acid	10	5	50.0
Folacin	0.3	0.1	66.7
Tocopherol	16	2.2	86.3
Betaine	844	650	22.8
Choline	1089	767	29.5
Calcium %	0.045	0.018	60.0
Phosphorus %	0.433	0.126	70.9
Magnesium %	0.183	0.028	84.7
Potassium %	0.454	0.105	77.0
Manganese, ppm	46	6.5	85.8
Iron, ppm	43	10.5	75.6
Zinc, ppm	35	7.8	77.7

I shudder to think of the siege of Leningrad. I was about 30 years old then with three small children. What a nightmare to think of being there during those three years—waiting in line at food service institutions for watery soup and knowing that many resorted to eating the flesh of those who died of malnutrition.

Fortunately, we can forget about such unthinkable happenings and go to our kitchens and prepare food to the hum of mills, mixers, juicers and blenders, and the convenience of graters, grinders, slicers, cookers, canners and dehydrators.

1. Adapted from Schroeder, H.A., "BBC Nutrition and Physical Fitness," American Journal Clinical Nutrition, 24:56, 1971, p. 131. Book No. 13.

Chapter 13

Recipes

Soups

IN SOUTH AMERICA AND OTHER COUN-TRIES, you have not had a meal until you have had a bowl of soup. But the day may come when soup will be the first and last course.

The simplicity of serving a bowl of soup, bread and a salad appeals to me now and for a future time of scarcities. When I think of a one-dish soup meal, I think of a family on Squatters Hill in Hong Kong, China. About sundown a pleasant young mother walked from her home (a shack), carefully holding onto a large bowl full of soup. She was carrying it to the main wide steps leading up the hill where her husband and two children waited. They had an overturned box for a table covered with a clean cloth where they ate their evening meal of soup.

Or, I think of Scotland where we came in out of the howling, blustery wind and rain to get warmed up with a bowl of "soup of the day" in a restaurant.

Advantages of soup — (a) It is economical. (b) It is a good vehicle to carry small amounts of various foods, where alone these may not be adequate or in acceptable portions. (c) Soup makes it easier for a large family to share and share alike (pieces of chicken cut up in a soup, for example). (d) It takes less pots and pans, serving dishes and fuel than most other menus. (f) It can be prepared ahead and eliminates the anxiety of keeping things warm while a big family gathers around.

Soup stock — Soup making begins with the stock. It is not much of a problem if you use a beef shin bone or soup bone sawed up in pieces. Scoop out the marrow and gently melt it. Put this and the bones and any vegetables (first or second class) you have around, such as carrots, celery, onions, outer leaves of vegetables (that you discard later) in a big pot. Cover with *cold* water. (Cold water draws the flavor out of the bones and vegetables; hot water holds them in.) Some cooks add two tablespoons of vinegar per quart of water to help dissolve the calcium in soup bones.

Let the bones and vegetables simmer away for three hours or so. Then cool so you can lift a sheet of hardened fat off the top. In the winter we put the kettle out in the snow. Save the fat for soap. If you had a bucket of bones, it would be convenient to make a few gallons of stock and freeze it in milk cartons to use as needed. Then you would not have to start a day ahead to make soup.

After you have strained the soup and discarded the fat, bones and vegetables, you are ready to start anew on the soup of your choice.

What if you do not have any soup bones? Do not despair. Make your soup like the vegetarians do. Omit the greasy soup bones and add a little butter, oil, cream or nut butter to the strained vegetable stock. If you do not have the usual vegetables you want to discard, make your stock using comfrey, mint, alfalfa, bran water, or gluten water. To get a meat flavor without meat, use the concentrated seasonings (ham, chicken or beef in liquid, powder, cube or paste form) of vegetable or animal origin.

Good looking soup — Make your clear soup clear and clean looking. No one likes unidentified bits of things floating in the soup. Cutting vegetables is a very important art. Do not cut all the vegetables the same size and the same shape. Vary them a little—big and little, round and square, long and thin, short and fat. But stick to uniform sizes for the individual vegetables. *Garnish the soup* with alfalfa sprouts, watercress, parsley, chives, grated carrot, beets, paper thin radishes, cucumber slices, shredded cheese or hard boiled eggs, chopped nuts, sesame seed or baco bits. Try popcorn, a lemon slice, paprika, diced pimento, raw celery, diced green pepper or okra slices.

Soups Using Legumes and Grains

Soy Bean Soup — A hearty change.

1 quart rich soup stock   3 cups cooked soy beans

Blend 2 cups of the stock with 1½ cups of the beans until smooth. Add the rest of the beans whole.

Add cut steamed vegetables:

2 carrots	1 garlic clove
1 green pepper	2 cups tomatoes
2 onions	2 ribs of celery
Add:	
2 Tbsp. oil	Salt and pepper

Try: Season thick soy milk with beef bouillon for a creamy soup (for thick milk use 1 cup soaked beans to 2-3 cups water in a blender and strain).

Start to season the soup with 1½ tsp. salt, 1 tsp. thyme and 1 Tbsp. chopped parsley. If it is too bland, add: 1 tsp. each garlic and onion powder, 2 tsp. celery powder, 2 or 3 bay leaves, ¼ tsp. each cayenne and paprika and ⅔ cup catsup or ½ cup tomato paste. Heat and serve.

Lentil Soup — An old favorite.

1 quart soup stock	2 carrots
1 cup dry lentils (no soaking necessary)	2 onions
⅓ cup brown rice flour for thickening (grind the rice in a seed mill or liquify)	2 ribs of celery and leaves
	3 garlic cloves

Steam all together 45 minutes one pan inside another (See page 29, *Passport to Survival*).

*Before serving, add 1 Tbsp. each olive oil and butter, 2 Tbsp. chopped parsley, 1½ tsp. salt, 3 Tbsp. brewers yeast.

Variations: For added protein, blend part of the lentils with ½ cup or more of nuts. Add diced parsnips or potatoes, soy noodles or millet. Add 1 tsp. lemon juice or some sour cream, a pinch of thyme, a bay leaf, tarragon or celery seed. (Wouldn't a ham bone with big chunks of ham in this taste good, or some ham soup base in the soup stock?)

(*Note:* I know you are wondering why I make lentil soup this way—The lentils cook quicker without salt. The oil, yeast and parsley are better for us if not subject to high heat, the rice for better protein balance. This small amount of soup can be cooked in the same bowl it is served in, with no burning, stirring or watching.)

Whole Dry Pea Soup —
A variation cheaper and better than split peas,
yet tastes the same.

2 cups soaked Alaska peas   3 cups soup stock
(soak about 12 hours)   1½ tsp. salt
Simmer one hour to soften

Blend until smooth. Add steamed chopped vegetables: a large carrot, an onion, 2 ribs of celery and a half a turnip (the other half is sure to be wormy!)

Season with a bay leaf, ¼ tsp. chervil or parsley, ½ tsp. savory. Add 1 cup of cream or canned milk. Variation: Omit vegetables and add minced onion and baco bits.

Note: For instant soup, grind whole peas into powder and sift into boiling stock to thicken. Add remaining ingredients.

Lima Bean Soup — For hearty eaters.

1 quart stock   1½ cups cooked millet
2½ cups cooked beans   or rice (¼ cup dry)
(limas or any other kind)
(1 cup dry)

Add lightly-cooked cut vegetables: 1 cup each tomatoes, onions and greens, ½ cup each carrots and celery, 3 Tbsp. parsley. Add ¼ cup oil and season with ½ tsp. sage, 1 tsp. caraway seed, 3 Tbsp. or less nutritional[1] yeast, a pinch of nutmeg; garnish with grated cheese.

Other seasonings that could be used: ¼ tsp. thyme, ½ clove garlic, lemon juice and bay leaf.

Lentil Rice-Tomato Soup

2 Tbsp. oil   4 cups water
1 med. onion, chopped   1 can tomatoes (#2)
1 cup dry lentils   ½ can tomato paste
½ cup natural rice, uncooked   1 cup tomato puree
Salt to taste   pinch sweet basil

----

1. Nutritional yeast was formerly called brewers yeast, a non-leavening yeast. It does not require refrigeration. Keep in a covered jar away from light.

Saute onion in oil. Add lentils, rice and water. Bring to boil, simmer until soft. Add tomatoes, salt and sweet basil. Add water if it is too thick.

Wheat Soup

2 cups each soup stock
  and milk

2 cups each, cooked wheat
  and carrots (cubed)

Heat the milk and soup stock. Thicken with cooked garbanzos. Blend smooth or press through sieve. Season with mushrooms, bay leaf, parsley, onion and garlic.

Minestrone Soup
(one gallon) A meal in itself.

Dice 2 quarts of vegetables: 1 cup each of carrots, potatoes, peas, zucchini, onions (or part leeks); 2½ cups tomatoes, ½ cup celery. Steam lightly. Add 1½ cups each, soy beans and rice, cooked. Add all ingredients to 2 quarts chicken stock. Add ¼ cup butter.

Season soup with:

1 tsp. salt
¼ tsp. pepper
2 tsp. dried parsley
½ tsp. chopped garlic

1 bay leaf
1 tsp. rosemary
1 tsp. basil

Garnish soup with fresh parsley and Parmeson cheese.
Variation: 1 cup cooked spaghetti.

Egg Dumplings

Beat 2 large eggs and add ⅓ cups flour and ¼ tsp. salt. Drop small bits off spoon into hot soup; cover and simmer.

Three "Easy on the Budget" Soups

1. Fresh Asparagus Soup

1½ cups raw asparagus, sliced
2 cups milk

1 chopped onion
1 can mushroom soup

Blend ½ the asparagus in the milk; strain out fiber. Tenderize remaining asparagus and onion. Combine all ingredients.

2. Missionary Soup

Hot tomato juice and a little butter and salt, loaded with fresh vegetables in season. This was the daily diet of two missionaries for a period of time. They felt great!

3. Plain Tomato Soup ı

To keep from curdling, use ¼ more milk than tomato juice and heat in separate pans. Add a little butter and honey to the tomato juice. Pour tomato juice quickly into milk. Season with salt and a pinch of nutmeg.

Beet Borsht
(Beautiful and perfect for summer.)

2 cups raw diced beets	1 green onion
2 cups sour cream	

Blend and season with kelp. (Cook the beets slightly before blending if desired.) Garnish with finely chopped parsley, lemon juice and salt to taste.

Borsht Variations

Combine: 1 quart stock with 1 cup previously made beet juice and 1 cup yogurt. Blend until smooth. Add 1 cup cooked diced beets and season with juice of one lemon, ½ tsp. salt, ½ tsp. tarragon or cloves, dill, allspice or bay leaves.

Green Soups — Something different.

Spinach

3 cups beef stock and 1 Tbsp. butter. Blend with 2 cups packed spinach slightly steamed. Add 1½ tsp. each honey and vinegar. Garnish with sour cream or blend in the sour cream. (Chopped avocado in the soup is good.)

Green Vegetable Soup

Combine asparagus, onions, spinach and parsley. Blend with soup stock and thicken with lima bean flour or arrowroot. Add a little oil and salt.

Different Soup-Making Techniques

The recipes given here have departed from the customary throw-everything-in-one-pot method of years gone by. To save nutrients, some of the ingredients are raw and some cooked, or vegetables are cooked separately to avoid overcooking. To a plain cream soup (like thin white sauce), the juice from asparagus, spinach, parsley, wheat grass, lettuce and other leafy greens could be added. Use about 2 Tbsp. of raw vegetable juice to 1 cup of cream soup. (Strain the juice first.) Soups can be thickened many ways, other than with flour. Use a blender to make a puree from potatoes, carrots, peas, beans, corn, barley, rice, millet, garbanzos and use to thicken the soup.

Examples of Simple Cream Soups

Creamed Millet Soup

1 part millet, 4 parts milk; steam for 1 hour. Blend until smooth or press through a strainer. Season to taste.

Corn Soup

Blend corn, milk and onion. Strain and season.

Carrot Soup

Dice three large carrots, an onion, and steam lightly. Blend ⅔ of them in 3 cups soup stock and ½ cup dry milk powder. Add ⅓ of the reserved cubed carrots. Season with salt, dill and parsley.

Corn and Potatoes

Cream together.

Nut Butter Soups

Add nut butter (or ground nuts) to cream soups including asparagus, corn, lima beans, peas, tomato, spinach.

Bean and Noodle Soup

Kidney bean puree thinned down to soup consistency. Add cooked noodles or add onion, celery, tomato, cabbage and parsley. Season with basil and serve with cheese.

Tomato Soup and Chopped Peanuts

Blend tomatoes. Heat and add finely-chopped peanuts, green peppers, celery and parsley.

Instant Potato Soup

Juice potatoes, celery, onion and peppers. Heat and stir until thick. (The starch in the potato thickens it.)

Salads

Our salads in the fall are platters of sliced tomatoes and green peppers and cucumbers. The winter and spring are our seasons for tossed salads.

Every family seems to have an established custom as to quantity of fresh vegetables to serve. One family reports using about ten pounds of fresh tomatoes a day when in season. Another family I visited passed a plate of sliced tomatoes (the first of the season), and each took a slice.

Tossed Salad

I begin my salads in the conventional way—in a big, cold garlic rubbed bowl. I break up crisp lettuce and add darker green leafy varieties and the usual celery, onions and radishes, using only thin slices of more expensive tomatoes and peppers standing by as a garnish. At this point, I depart from restaurant-type salads and add anything fresh I have, such as:

Sunflower greens	Snips of new carrot or
Buckwheat greens	radish tops
Wheat grass greens	Comfrey or sour dock
Asparagus tips, raw	Raw cauliflower pieces
Alfalfa sprouts	and leaves
Bean sprouts	Fresh mushrooms, sliced thin
Cold cooked millet	A few sprouted lentils
Strips of gluten	Pieces of red smoked salmon,
Sesame seeds or nuts	tuna or shrimp
Tender new dandelion leaves	Cubes of meat and/or cheese

Garnish with a swirl of avocado slices (dipped in lemon juice), cherry tomatoes, pickles, eggs, a sprinkle of fresh alfalfa, or sprouts around the edge. Serve with crisp sesame covered bread sticks and a glass of milk. Have a choice of dressings on the table, to suit individual tastes. People like to know what they are eating. Chop the celery and chives if you like, but leave the buckwheat and sunflower greens whole.

A finely-chopped salad is a heavy, dense, wet one. Work fast and have a loose, light crisp one. Put all your salad-making ingredients together on one shelf of the refrigerator. If they are in one container, you may lift them out all at once. Use long celery crispers and plastic bags. There will be no limp vegetables in this gourmet salad. (If prepared before serving time, cover and refrigerate the salad or place over a bowl of ice.)

Raw Salad Plate

People today are using more raw vegetables than just cole slaw, grated carrots, waldorf or lettuce salad. Salad plates have more variety than just radish roses, carrot curls and celery sticks. Now people are enjoying:

Raw beet and potato sticks   Broccoli
Zucchini slices   Spinach
Corn on the cob, raw   Tiny string beans
Brussel sprouts

The appeal for raw vegetables comes from growing your own and having them from the garden to the table in ten minutes.

Raw Rainbow Salad

The first new beets, green and red cabbage, kohlrabi, parsley and carrots look pretty for a company dinner when grated fine and placed in a rainbow of separate colors on a large salad platter (see photo). Make a fringe of water cress around the edge. Have vegetables clean and cold and grate them just before the guests are seated. Pass a tray with salad dressings and toppings for those who want them — coconut, raisins, dates, nuts, pineapple cubes, orange slices or banana slices dipped in grated

Rainbow salad: grated beets, cabbage, kohlrabi, parsley and carrots.

nuts. (It does not sound much like survival food!) Serve with cold carrot juice as a drink.

Cabbage Salad

Heat and mix ¾ cup honey with 1 cup vinegar. Cool; then add 1 tsp. celery seed, 1 tsp. mustard seeds or 1 tsp. prepared mustard, 1 tsp. salt, ¼ cup chopped onion, ⅓ cup chopped green pepper, ½ cup finely chopped carrots or ½ cup chopped red pepper, 2½ pound head cabbage, shredded. Chill combination in refrigerator for one hour. This salad can be stored in a covered container in refrigerator for several days. It will retain its crispness.

Mock Crab Salad

Grate turnips in long shreds. Break up the crisp white part of the lettuce into bite-sized pieces. Mix in some canned salmon or tuna. Serve on a lettuce leaf with a dressing.

Cabbage Leaf Roll

Mix 1 cup diced apples, ½ cup ground nuts, ½ cup raisins or dates, ¼ cup minced parsley. Roll mixture in a cabbage leaf.

Vegetable salad boats.

Salad Boats

Raw salad boats with various fillings are always pretty in a nest of greens. A tomato can be scooped out or a pepper, turnip, cucumber, kohlrabi, or zucchini. (See photo at bottom of page 136.)

Cooked salad boats could be: beets, potatoes, eggplant or squash. Fruit boats from apples, pineapple, melons, oranges or bananas are interesting.

Fillings—for vegetable boats could be:

1. **Raw corn** cut off the cob, tossed together with grated coconut and a dressing.

2. **Soy beans** — equal amounts of cooked soy beans, chopped celery, shredded carrots, minced onion garnished with green peppers. A dressing of equal amounts of mayonnaise and sour cream, seasoned with onion and garlic powder, parsley, sea salt (or a seasoned salt).

Mungbean sprouts — long—marinate in:

¼ cup oil   2 Tbsp. vinegar
2 Tbsp. soy sauce

Chop and add:

¼ cup pimento   ¼ cup onion and 1 clove garlic

Sprinkle 2 Tbsp. sesame seed over the top.

Alfalfa sprouts, fine grated carrots and minced celery.

Avocado mashed with ground nuts or chopped boiled eggs and onion (This is also good on toast.)

Lentil filling — 2 cups lentils cooked and mashed; add ½ cup sunflower seed and ½ cup ground nuts, seasoning.

Soy bean — Cook and grind soy beans. (I use a Champion juicer and they come out smooth as butter by putting the beans through a time or two.) Season to taste with onion, garlic or salad seasonings. This is good to stuff celery or pepper slices.

Variation: 2 cups cooked mashed soy beans, 1 cup ground gluten, or meat, ¼ cup chopped steamed onions, ½ tsp. salt. Moisten if needed with catsup. Chopped nuts (¼ cup) could be added if available.

Raw beets — This relish is good to fill a cooked beet boat. Four cups beets, ground or shredded—marinated in ⅓ cup each of lemon juice, oil and honey. Season with 2 Tbsp. soy sauce, 2 tsp. horseradish, ½ tsp. each of cloves and allspice. (Red cabbage is good as a substitute for part of the beets.)

Cooked beets — In Europe all the beets I saw in the markets were pre-cooked. They blend well with chopped salted peanuts in a salad on a bed of greens.

Marinated Salad

Soy Salad

3 cups hot cooked
  soy beans
½ cup oil

½ cup vinegar, or
  lemon juice
2 Tbsp. fresh dill

Marinate overnight; add chopped vegetables and chill.
Variation: Use cooked garbanzos in place of soy beans. Chop ½ cup each of celery, onion and green pepper. Add 2 Tbsp. parsley and 1 clove garlic.

Garbanzos — sweet sour—marinate in equal portions of honey, oil and vinegar.

Bean salad — 1 cup each of cooked green beans, wax beans, kidney beans, garbanzos, raw cauliflowerettes, and sliced raw onion. Marinate overnight in French dressing.

Dilled carrots — 2 cups cooked steamed baby carrots, marinated in ⅓ cup each of salad oil and lemon juice, 1 tsp. or more of honey, 2 Tbsp. chopped dill, 1 tsp. salt, 1 garlic clove.

Zucchini salad — Slice two medium zucchini and steam lightly for five minutes. Marinate in ½ cup oil, ⅔ cup vinegar, 1Tbsp. each chopped onion and fresh mint leaves. Chill. Add salt.

Cauliflower — Tenderize 2 cups cauliflower and 1 cup each carrots and peas. Add cubes of dill pickle and meat or gluten and some mayonnaise. Chill.

Asparagus — 1 pound of asparagus. Cut and tenderize. Marinate in 4 Tbsp. lemon juice, 6 Tbsp. oil, 3 Tbsp. honey, ¼ tsp. each of oregano, thyme, tarragon, a bit of garlic and ½ tsp. salt.

Main Dish Salad

Tuna wheat — or millet salad (A family favorite)

4 cups of steamed cracked wheat *(see note below)	¼ cup green peppers, chopped
1 cup of tuna (or any meat)	2 cups of dressing—Mayonnaise and catsup
1 cup celery	mixed is good.
½ cup green onion	

*Note: Wheat or millet is equally good, but steam it in less water than usual so you have loose light individual kernels not soft mush. The drier kernels will soak up more dressing and taste better. Other things can be added to this salad, such as sweet pickle relish and radishes mixed in with the wheat. Garnish with olives, egg slices, cheese cubes, parsley, pickle slices, or whatever you have. (This salad is great as a stuffing for tomatoes.)

Beverages

Good cold water that flows down to us from springs and melting snow on the mountains is one of our best beverages. Why then do we need more kinds of drinks? The obvious reasons are: (a) Many people at home and abroad are not fortunate enough to get clean safe water. (b) Fruit and vegetable juices or herb teas help us get our quota of 6 to 7 cups of fluid a day. (c) Nutritious drinks help young, old, sick and well get food that is easily assimilated and often more acceptable. (d) Wholesome beverages can replace harmful ones. In the traditional friendly custom of "sipping" together or as group refreshments, one group of 350 youth enjoyed hot mint tea sweetened with honey. (Mint was fresh from their own gardens.) (e) Hot beverages may impart a sense of comfort and cheeriness in troubled times.

Mint tea — Drop a quart or more of fresh mint leaves in a gallon of boiling water. Cover and let stand 20 minutes. Strain and add honey to taste. (Never boil tea. Aromatic properties evaporate and some nutrients are destroyed.)

Variation: Use mixed wild edible greens instead of mint.

Hot Dark Drinks

These can be made from various parched or (burned) foods like wheat, barley, sweet potato, white potato, and many more things. (See toastum drink made from parched wheat on page 65, *Passport to Survival*.) A good variation of this for a party is 1 Tbsp. toastum (parched powdered wheat) to 2 cups boiling water. Simmer and add 2 tsp. honey, 3 Tbsp. canned milk, 1 tsp. instant cocoa (or carob), ¼ tsp. nutmeg and ¼ tsp. vanilla.

Other Nutritious Drinks

Soy milk — The soaked beans should be cooked about 30 minutes before being blended. Use 1 cup cooked beans to 1 quart of water. Blend at high speed about 5 minutes. (Less water in the blender can be used and the remainder added later.) A pinch of salt, drop of lemon, a tsp. of honey improves the flavor. (If soy milk is used over a long period of time, you may want to supplement it with some iron and calcium phosphate. (See proteins.)

Whey — From making cheese or purchased in powder form. 1 Tbsp. of whey powder comes from nearly 2 quarts of liquid whey. (I am going to dry and powder my acidophilus.) Whey is used with pineapple juice for a drink or used in place of milk in other drinks. It is also used in baking.

Rejuvelac—wheat cider — As mentioned, this is a beneficial ferment! 1 cup wheat, 2 cups water. Soak 24 hours. Pour off water and stand at room temperature a day or more until it bubbles. (Use the wheat for planting or cooking.) The liquid tastes like whey and provides friendly bacteria for healthy intestinal flora.

Variation: Soak wheat for 4 days, put in refrigerator. Each time you pour off a cup of water to drink, replace it. The wheat will keep for weeks.

Green drinks in the spring are now a routine part of our diet There are many green drink formulas. We use whatever leaves are tender and fresh. The alfalfa, comfrey, and dandelion leaves are first in the spring; later parsley, spinach, and celery leaves are used. Add enough water in the blender so the blades will turn. Strain and add equal amounts of pineapple juice. If not available, blend apples with the greens (or drink it plain—try a drink of milk for a 'chaser.')

Wheat grass — Used alone or in combination with other greens is a powerful blood builder. It is grown in flats or trays. (Cut when 5 or 6 inches high and grind in a meat grinder or a special grass juice grinder. Or it could be chopped and put in the blender with other greens.)

Vegetable cubes — One fall I froze a gallon of vegetable juice in trays (made 82 cubes). It was convenient in the winter to use for green drinks in the blender or with hot seasoned milk for a soup. I used:

spinach	dandelion	chard
parsley	sour dock	rutabaga tops
beet tops	turnip tops	chicory leaves
carrot tops	onions	
lettuce	comfrey	

Mineral broth — (Like a hot soup.) Make from grinding carrots, celery, onions, parsley and spinach. Steam lightly then cover with equal parts hot tomato juice and water. Let stand 6 hours, strain and drink hot or cold.

Fruit Drink

Banana drink — If you have a blender and 2 cups of milk, a banana, an egg, a cup of berries and a little honey, you have a good drink. Ice cubes in the blender make it more of a sherbet texture.

Interesting Drink Ideas from Mexico

1. Thicken starch water from gluten very slightly. Add milk and blended frozen fruit.

2. Can use oatmeal water. (Pour water over oatmeal.) Also use rice water the same way, seasoned with cinnamon and nutmeg.

3. Dry orange peels and make a tea by boiling cinnamon sticks with them. Sweeten to taste.

4. Put cantaloupe seeds in the blender. Add 2 cups water and sugar. Strain and drink.

Argenta Liquado — (Like our low-calorie milkshake.) 8 oz. liquid, 4 or 5 ice cubes and a piece of fruit: banana, apple, plum, pineapple, peach, apricot. Honey to sweeten.

Grain, Legume, and Vegetable Dishes

Meatless Patties

One-half cup each: lentils, garbanzos, dry peas, walnuts, bread crumbs, celery and onions combined. Soak the legumes and grind with the other ingredients. Season with beef soup mix flavoring. This makes 24 small patties. (I use an ice cream scoop, cutting each one in fourths.) Serve this with a salad and a grain dish either steamed wheat, millet or rice pudding.

Meatless Pattie #2

One-half cup each dry rice, millet, lentils. Cover with 3 cups of water and steam 45 minutes. Add ½ cup each ground nuts and bread crumbs. Season with 1 Tbsp. chopped garlic, 1 tsp. salt, 1 tsp. sage, ¼ tsp. ground celery seed. Makes five cups of mixture and 30 patties. Cook as desired.

Rice and Soy Patties (no eggs)

2 cups cooked mashed
  soybeans
1 cup cooked rice
½ cup bread crumbs

¼ cup dry milk powder
1 cup tomato juice
  (or enough to moisten
  mixture)

Season with: 2 Tbsp. chopped onion, 1 tsp. thyme, and 1 tsp. oregano. Bake in loaf about 45 minutes at 350°, or make into patties.

Soy Nut Loaf

2 cups cooked soybeans
1 cup cooked whole oats

2 cups raw peanuts,
  grind

Season with ½ cup chopped onion, ½ tsp. sage, 2-4 Tbsp. beef style seasoning. Add enough tomato juice to moisten; bake in shallow baking dish and serve in squares.

Chili

2 quarts sprouted,
  cooked beans
1 ½ quarts ground baked
  gluten
3 quarts tomato juice
  (or 2 cans tomato sauce
  thinned down)
⅓ cup oil

2 each: large onions and
  peppers, chopped
3 Tbsp. honey
1 pkg. chili seasoning
1 ½ Tbsp. chili powder
4 beef bouillon cubes,
  dissolved in ¼ cup water
1 Tbsp. cumin

Try: carob or chocolate (1 ounce to 1 quart cooked beans).

Wheat Sprout Balls

2 cups sprouted wheat
  and 1 large onion
  ground together

Add: ½ cup peanut butter
      1 ¼ cups bread crumbs
      1 cup milk
      2 Tbsp. oil
      1 tsp. salt

Form into balls (about 3 dozen). Bake at 400° for 15 minutes.
Variations: Add 1 cup ground nuts in place of peanut butter. Use soy flour, brewers yeast, garbanzo flour in place of part of the bread crumbs.

Lunch Meat

Use equal parts ground meat, cracked soaked wheat and nuts, grind together, season as for meat load. Press tightly in round juice cans and bake until firm. Slice very thin.

Wheat Ideas

Use cracked or whole wheat in place of rice. Use it in Spanish dishes, stuffed peppers, sloppy Joe's, in vegetable soups, in applesauce cake, frozen desserts. (However, I rebel when I see sprouted wheat mixed with fruit salad. I think there are less obvious ways to use it.)

Lima Bean and Soy Cheese (Tofu)
(See pages 160, 161, and 162 for making Tofu)

2½ cups cooked limas   ¼ cup butter
1 cup soy cheese, cubed   ½ tsp. each: basil, thyme
½ cup chopped parsley   and salt

Bake in casserole dish at 350° for 30 minutes.

Lima Beans, Potatoes and Corn

2 cups cooked lima beans   1 cup diced potatoes,
2 cups milk   steamed with ½ cup each:
¾ tsp. salt   corn and onion
1 tsp. butter

Tofu Cooking and Uses

Tofu Patties

1 cup tofu, mashed   2 Tbsp. brewers yeast
1 egg   ½ cup chopped green pepper
½ cup bread crumbs   ¼ cup parsley

Season with ½ tsp. each: soy sauce, Italian seasoning, celery salt, chicken seasoning, pinch of garlic salt. Heat patties and serve with tomato gravy.

More Ideas for Using Soy Beans
Tofu Variations

—When stuffing potatoes, use 1 part tofu to 3 parts potato.
—Place 2 cups tofu cubes in a can of tomato soup, adding 2 Tbsp. each: oil, celery, onion and green pepper. (If cheese is crumbly, blend it with the soup before adding other ingredients.)

—Patties—equal parts tofu, nuts and grated carrots or equal parts tofu, rice and seasoned bread crumbs.
—Add tofu to scrambled eggs.
—Use tofu with ripe olives or pimento for a sandwich spread.
—Stretch Parmesan cheese by adding tofu. (We dried tofu and powdered it and started adding it to Parmesan cheese until we reached the proportion of 1 part Parmesan cheese to 8 parts tofu.)
—Basic seasoning for tofu is soy sauce, celery salt, green onions, tomato sauce or paste, vegetable or meat bouillon cubes.
—Mix tofu with tuna, gluten or ground meat for a pattie, using an egg, onion, celery, peppers for seasoning.
—See other recipes in the candy and dessert section.

Soy Spread

3 cups cooked soybeans, pressed through a sieve. Season with 1 medium onion and ¼ cup finely chopped parsley, 1 Tbsp. soy sauce, ¼ tsp. basil, 1½ tsp. cumin. Serve on toast or use to stuff celery.

Soy Dips

Thin soy spread with cream for a dip. Sour cream, garlic and mustard could be added.

Soy Dip #2

Use 1½ cups soy residue (after straining soy milk for tofu, page 161), ¾ cup sour cream. Season with 1½ tsp. onion salt, ¼ tsp. garlic powder, 1 tsp. mustard, lemon or vinegar to taste. Other vegetable seasoning could be used.

Soy Nuts

1½ cups soybeans soaked overnight. Sprinkle 1½ tsp. salt over the bottom of a large shallow pan. Spread beans over salt in a single layer. Lightly sprinkle more salt over top of beans and roast uncovered in a 350° oven for 45 minutes, stirring often until beans are evenly browned and crisp. (I wondered if the salt helped draw the moisture out of the beans. Without deep fat frying, it is hard to get the beans crunchy.)

Vegetables — Good Combinations and Ways to Serve

Most of us are happy with the plain flavor of fresh garden vegetables. But for variety try the following:

Edible Pod Peas

1 pound green edible pod peas, steamed—serve with egg butter; 2 hard cooked eggs pressed through a strainer; 4 Tbsp. soft butter and 1 Tbsp. minced green onion; salt to taste.

Cabbage with Sour Cream

Cabbage (and Brussels sprouts) are good when cooked lightly and covered with soup cream and sprinkled with dill seed.

Spinach with Cream and Nutmeg

Chopped, cooked spinach served with thick cream and a pinch of nutmeg is yummy!

Broiled Tomatoes

Over firm slices of tomatoes in a broiler pan, sprinkle: salt, pepper, sugar, Worcestershire sauce and dots of butter. Cover lightly with bread crumbs. Broil about 5 minutes.

Zucchini Casserole

Slice and steam 3 medium zucchini for 10 minutes. Arrange in casserole and cover with white sauce to which has been added: chopped green onion, parsley and cubed mild cheese. Top with buttered bread crumbs. Heat through in oven 350° for 30 minutes. Make plenty.

Cabbage and onions served with butter and toasted sesame seed.

Casserole — Celery, green pepper, onion, garlic, mushroom soup. (Four parts celery, 1 part combined: onion, pepper and garlic.)

Celery, onion and green pepper (in that order of quantity) is good seasoning for cooked rice, wheat, mung sprouts, millet, lentils, barley, rye, etc.

Onions with limas: pour over white sauce seasoned with thyme.

Vegetables and scrambled eggs — eggplant, green peppers, tomatoes, zucchini, onions, garlic, olive oil and salt and pepper. Serve with scrambled eggs.

Zucchini with tomatoes — six cups zucchini sliced, 3 cups chopped tomatoes. Season with thyme, garlic, basil or oregano, salt and sugar.

Corn chowder — cooked cubed potatoes, onions sauteed lightly (not brown) and creamed corn. Add milk or light cream and salt to taste.

Baked squash and fruit — cover serving-size pieces of hard squash with a fruit sauce from apples, pears, peaches or apricots. Bake as usual.

Vegetable Roll-ups and Filled "Boats"

Stuffed Peppers

Serve rice, onions and tomatoes in raw peppers, or fill them with soy cheese, diced celery, alfalfa sprouts (seasoned with kelp instead of salt). Cooked stuffed peppers: fill with ground gluten, rice and onions. Bake 350° for 30 minutes.

Stuffed Baked Onions

Parboil onions, scoop out center, fill with ground gluten or sausage.

Tomato—Poached Egg

Scoop out center of ripe tomato. Break an egg in it and bake only long enough to set egg.

Cabbage Roll

Steam 6 large cabbage leaves. Fill with:

1 can tuna fish*	1 Tbsp. sesame seed
*(or beef-flavored gluten)	1 Tbsp. prepared mustard

1 cup cooked rice   1 egg
½ cup celery   ¼ cup onion
2 Tbsp. parsley

Cover and bake at 350° for 30 minutes. Mix 2 cups tomato sauce with 1 cup sour cream. Heat and spoon over the cabbage rolls.

Beet Cups

Fill cooked beets (that have been scooped out) with chopped cooked greens and hard cooked eggs; add a little lemon juice and salt.

Stuffed Acorn Squash

(A half squash.) Fill with nut loaf mixture seasoned with sage. Bake.

French Fried Parsnips

Dip cooked parsnip slices in egg and bread crumbs and fry.

Loaves and Patties—Vegetables, Nuts and Cheese

Vegetable Loaf

Mix 2 cups cooked brown rice with ½ cup each: carrots, onion, celery, green peas, parsley, 1 garlic clove (minced), an egg and a little oil. Salt to taste. Bake covered at 350° for 45 minutes.

Carrot Patties

Grind 12 small carrots, 1 onion and a stalk of celery; add an egg and enough cornmeal to form into patties. Fry and serve with cheese on top.

Broccoli Stem Patties

Two cups broccoli stem, pealed and chopped, 1 chopped green onion, ¼ cup peanut butter. Form into patties. Bake and serve with chili sauce or tomato sauce.
    Variation: Before baking, sprinkle 1 cup crumbled tofu on top.

Vegetable Souffle

1 pound of any garden greens, chopped	1 ½ cups grated cheese
½ onion	½ tsp. each oregano
4 eggs, beaten	and basil
	Salt to taste

Combine and bake in covered dish 325° for 35 minutes. Tofu could be used in place of grated cheese.

Using Mung Sprouts, Comfrey, Dandelion, and Jerusalem Artichoke

Long Mung Bean Sprouts—Ways to Serve Them

Dice 1 ½ cups celery, 1 cup onions, ¾ cup green pepper. Steam until partly done (still green and crisp). Add 3 cups mung sprouts; cover and simmer 5 or 10 minutes. Add 1 Tbsp. soy sauce or more. Thicken the vegetable juices and soy sauce, adding a little more water if desired. Serve over hot rice.

Variation: Warm long bean sprouts in butter. Add onion powder, salt and serve. Don't cook long enough to wilt bean sprouts. Add soy sauce last.

Soy Noodles

1 cup soy flour*	about 3 Tbsp. water**
1 egg	1 Tbsp. oil
½ tsp. salt	

—Mix into a soft dough.
—Press out with the hands on a heavily floured board, sprinkling more flour over the top so it can be rolled out very thin with a rolling pin.
—Air dry for an hour or so depending on the humidity.
—Dust surface of dough with flour.
—Roll up loosely like jelly roll and cut in ¼ inch slices.
—Shake out and drop in soup or salted water.
—Cook for 10 to 15 minutes.

 * In place of all soy flour use half whole wheat, or barley.
 ** Use juice from spinach, beets, or carrots for a colorful noodle. (Vary the shape of the noodles: tiny squares or animal cut-outs.)

Mashed Potatoes and Sprouts

Make a sandwich using mashed potato for the top and bottom* layer and a mixture of chopped mung sprouts, peanuts, cooked soy beans, a little soy sauce, onion salt, held together with a little of the mashed potato—for the filling. Or make a ball of the mashed potato and make a deep indentation with the thumb and fill with the sprout mixture, closing up again to form a ball.

* We used a pastry tube with mashed potato in it to form a decorative border around each sprout sandwich. Or form the potatoes in tiny balls to decorate the top—use red pimento, olives, etc. Form the potatoes and sprouts into patties, dip in egg and bake.

Using Comfrey in Meals

Greens

Fresh green comfrey leaves should be cooked with a minimum of water for about 10 minutes. Chinese wilt chopped comfrey leaves in warm butter until the leaves have shrunk and exuded enough juice; the use of water in cooking is unnecessary.

Comfrey 'Au Gratin'

Made with a layer of cooked rice on the bottom of a Pyrex dish. Alternate with layers of comfrey leaves, rice, grated cheese and dots of butter, ending with rice. Cover with a little milk or cream and bake at 350° about 30 minutes.

Comfrey Soup

Roll a few comfrey leaves very tightly and place them in your soup kettle, stew pot, or add to any meat or fish dish you are preparing. Add this during the last 10 minutes of cooking. Later lift the roll out with two forks. You have added valuable minerals to your food. Vegetarians make a soup of comfrey, potatoes, onions, nettles and season it with sage, thyme, savory and marjoram, adding an egg yolk and cream before serving. The ribs of the comfrey leaves and the stalky part of nettle is removed before cooking. (Comfrey can be frozen or dried for use when not in season.)

Dandelion Hot Cakes

Beat 3 medium eggs. Brown 3 medium chopped onions in oil. Mix eggs and onions. Cut one bunch of dandelion greens in pieces and boil. Add romono Italian cheese grated (4 or 5 Tbsp.). Heat pan and add 2 Tbsp. oil; form the above mixture into patties and cook slowly. (Dandelion flowers used in egg omelets are good.)

Jerusalem Artichokes (or Sunchokes)

This delicately-flavored vegetable is low in calories—only 22 calories per pound. They have 25% less fat than potatoes, double the calcium, 500 times as much iron with much more vitamin A and only 1/10th as much sodium.
  —For breakfast—Dice and add to scrambled eggs and bacon.
  —For lunch—Slice and add to salads.
  —For dinner—Dice, bake, boil, fry or mash. Cream them in a casserole, or use as a tasty extender in meat loaf.
  —Basic preparation—Boiled: Scrub tubers well in cold, running water, using a very stiff brush. Cook in boiling, salted water to cover for 10 to 12 minutes, or until just tender-crisp. If the tubers are quite large, they may take up to 5 minutes longer. *Don't overcook.* Remove sunchokes from the liquid, setting liquid aside to use in soups, aspics, or stews. Peel or rub the skin off the sunchokes and cut in cubes or slices. Season with melted butter, salt and pepper. One pound serves 3 to 4.

Sunchoke Casserole

4 cups boiled or mashed
  artichokes
½ cup melted butter

2 beaten eggs
2 cups fine bread crumbs

Bake 30 minutes in moderate oven.

Breads, Crackers and Crusts

Never-Fail Whole Wheat Bread

  1. Sprinkle: 2 Tbsp. yeast in ½ cup warm water (do not stir).

2. Mix well in order given:

> 5 cups hot water from tap
> ⅔ cup honey
> ⅔ cup cooking oil
> 2 Tbsp. salt
> 7 cups unsifted whole wheat flour

3. Add: Yeast (that has gone to the bottom and come up again in the warm water and is foamy on top); 5-6 more cups whole wheat flour; stir.

4. Pour ¼ of the dough at a time in a nest of flour. Combine the four balls and knead well for 5-10 minutes. Use only enough flour to keep from sticking. Oil may be used on the hands and board.

5. Divide into 6 sections (or into portions according to pan sizes). Shape into loaves and put in lightly-oiled pans. Let rise until dough is ⅓ higher than when first put in the pan. Bake at 350° for about 40 minutes. Brush top with butter and remove from pans. (With an electric wheat mill and bread mixer, author Beatrice Trum Hunter says it takes only about 15 minutes of her time (while working in the kitchen) to bake 18 loaves of bread.)

Beet Bread

Sprinkle:
  2 Tbsp. yeast in
  ½ cup warm water

Mix in order given:

2 cups hot water or	2 Tbsp. salt
beet liquid	5 cups whole wheat flour
½ cup oil	yeast
½ cup honey	5 more cups whole wheat flour

  Knead 5 to 10 minutes. Let rise ⅓.

Mix in blender:

½ cup hot water	½ cup flaxseed
2 cups cooked beets	2 Tbsp. dried parsley

Add: ½ cup soy flour

Combine with bread dough; knead again. Follow step 4 in basic recipe (try dried beet powder or dried squash powder.)

Norwegian Flat Bread

Cook and mash: 12 medium potatoes (about 3 lbs.)
Knead in: 2½ cups rye flour to make smooth paste
(Try drying out in dehydrator)
Stand one day. Press on floured board as thinly as possible. Form into cakes as large as can be handled. Turn several times with a pancake turner, while baking in a skillet. Serve with softened butter and sour cream and honey.

Corn Crisps
(Dried in sun or dehydrator, or 300° oven)

3 cups finely ground
   sweet corn

2 cups tomato juice
¼ cup oil

Season with: ¼ tsp. cayenne or less, ¼ tsp. curry, 1 clove garlic, 1 medium onion, minced. Mix and spread out in very thin sheets and dry until crisp. (For this and other unfried foods, see *Dry It, You'll Like It* by Macnman.)

Crisp Crackers

1½ cups whole wheat flour
⅓ cup oil
1 tsp. sugar

½ tsp. salt
⅓ cup water

Mix and add only enough water to make a firm dough. Roll out thin, cut square or round. Bake at 300° about 20 minutes.

Crisp Cracker Rings

½ cup each cornmeal,
   soy flour and
   millet flour

1 cup flour
2 cups water
3 Tbsp. oil

Season with: 2 tsp. salt, ¼ tsp. each garlic and onion powder, ½ cup Parmesan cheese.
Combine and strain through a fine strainer and use in a squirt bottle* to make oblong bite-size circles on a teflon cookie sheet. Bake at 350° about 10 minutes.
Simplified mixture for this: 1 cup water, 1 cup flour, ½ tsp. salt. (½ tsp. each garlic and onion powder if desired)
   * Instead of using a squirt bottle, pour the thin dough on a cookie sheet, pour off the excess and leave on even film. Bake until crisp and it lifts up from the cookie sheet. Optional: Score into 1½" squares when dough is partly cooked.

Millet Crackers (chewy)

½ cup ground millet flour   ¼ tsp. grated lemon rind
1 cup applesauce   ¼ tsp. salt
1 Tbsp. honey

Mix and drop spoonfulls on cookie sheet. Flatten slightly and bake in slow oven 300° for ½ hour or until firm. This can be spread ¼" thick on plastic wrap and dried in the sun or dehydrator.

Breakfasts—At Home and Abroad

Granola

Mix:
  1 cup sunflower seeds   ½ cup sesame seeds
  1 cup wheat germ   ½ cup flax seeds
  1 cup coconut (dry   1 cup soy flour
    and fine)   grated rind of 1 lemon

Combine with:
  ½ cup hot water   1 scant tsp. salt
  1 cup honey   2 tsp. vanilla
  ½ cup oil

Add:
  7 cups rolled oats

Place on cookie sheets. Bake at 200° to dry about 2 hours. Store in refrigerator when cool.

Hot Wheat Cereal

For about 10 years a family I know have eaten wheat cereal every morning cooked the same way: grind the wheat fine; run through hand grinder twice, add in proportions of 1 part grain to three parts water, adding the grain to cold water so it does not lump. Heat to a bubbly boil; put on lid and remove from heat. It is ready to eat in a few minutes. If the grain is overheated, it loses its sweet taste.

Hot Cakes Made With Yeast

Sprinkle:
   *2 Tbsp. yeast in
   ¼ cup water

Mix:
   3 Tbsp. oil   2 egg yolks
   2 Tbsp. honey   1½ cups hot tap water

Add:
   Softened yeast and 1½ cups sifted whole wheat flour, ¼ cup dry milk and ¾ tsp. salt.

   Mix and rise in warm place until double. Fold in 2 egg whites, beaten. (Substitute 1 Tbsp. baking powder for the yeast, if desired.)

   * Hot cakes mixed the night before will require just 1 Tbsp. yeast or add 3 Tbsp. and use immediately. For waffles, increase oil to ⅔ cup and use 3 eggs.

For a smaller quantity use:
   ¾ cup whole wheat flour   ¾ cup milk
   1½ tsp. baking powder   1½ Tbsp. oil
      (or 1 Tbsp. yeast)   1 egg
   ½ tsp. salt   1 Tbsp. honey

   Variations of basic hot cakes:

   Bread crumb griddle cakes — In the basic hot cake recipe above use 1½ cups stale bread crumbs soaked in 1½ cups water. Add just ½ cup flour and the remaining ingredients.

   Substitute rice polish, cornmeal, rye, buckwheat, soy, etc. for ½ the flour in hot cakes or waffles. Add wheat germ to batter (1 cup has 25.2 grams of protein, plus B vitamins, etc.) Use sour milk, buttermilk or yogurt instead of sweet milk. Add to batter: Fruits: blueberries, bananas, chopped apples, etc. Protein:

cheese, chicken, fish, nuts. Vegetables: onion, chives, garlic, spinach. Sprouts: soybean, wheat, etc.

Emergency Waffles—Surprisingly Good (eat while hot)

1 cup whole wheat flour   ½ tsp. salt
1 cup water

These take longer to bake—about 4 to 5 minutes. They are crisp and delicious. Serve with peanut butter and applesauce. If you are out of bread, this is a quick way to get a piece to eat with a salad, or use as a base for a creamed dish. (Makes 3 waffles, about 400 calories, 12 grams protein.)

Make sure waffle iron has been greased. Serve with hot honey and butter.

Up to ½ cup sunflower, pumpkin, flax or sesame seeds can be used in combinations with the grains.

Note: Any of the following or combinations of these may be used: rice, whole oats, barley, corn, buckwheat groats.

Alabama Staple

Mash bananas, add oatmeal and honey.

Birchermusesli (one-dish Swiss meal)

Mix together: Milk, yogurt, rolled oats and any fresh fruit in season.

Quick Breakfast

Mix in blender: One cup wheat sprouts, one cup water and a few dates. Grind in seed grinder: equal parts wheat and pumpkin seed; add dates.

Grot from Sweden

Stir whole wheat flour in boiling water to porridge consistency. Add salt to taste. When cold, it will be a soft jelly. In days gone by, only the wealthy could afford milk to pour over it. Try raisins, nuts, vanilla, etc.

Indian Breakfast

Use equal parts cracked wheat and cracked corn. For 2 servings, try 2 Tbsp. each grain. Sprinkle into 1 cup boiling water with ⅓ tsp. salt. Cook until thick. (Add dried fruit and nuts.)

Wheat Again

For a different flavor make cracked cooked wheat cereal from parched wheat. Steamed sprouted wheat (needs no water) is good with cream and honey.

Cookies, Candies and Desserts

Plain Cookies

Mix until creamy and smooth:
  ½ cup raw sugar   1 egg
  ½ cup butter

Add:
  1 ½ cups whole wheat flour   ⅓ tsp. salt

Chill and roll in small roll and cut in ½ inch pieces. Roll in a ball between hands and press flat. Bake at 350° for 10 minutes. Makes 4 dozen cookies.

Variations:

—Honey cookies—Use honey (or molasses) in place of sugar.
—Peanut butter cookies—Replace ½ of the butter with peanut butter.
—Filled cookies—Put ½ tsp. raisin, date, pear, or apricot between two thin cookies.
—Pinwheel cookies—Add carob to half the batter. Roll out thin. Place the dark and light dough together, roll up and cut with a string in small slices. Bake.
—Other additions to the basic recipe: Add coconut, nuts, spices, grated lemon or orange peel, sprouted wheat, mashed potatoes, etc.

Fudge You'll Like

Combine:
¼ cup hot water	¼ cup honey

Add:
½ cup sunflower seeds	1/8 cup carob
½ cup sunflower seed meal	any amount of nuts
½ cup coconut	

Mix together and spread out on parchment and dry in the sun, in dehydrator, or oven.

Corn Candy

Mix:
¼ cup honey	⅓ tsp. salt
2 Tbsp. peanut butter	

Chop coarsely and add:
⅓ cup sunflower seeds	⅓ cup raw peanuts

Add:
1 cup cornmeal

Form into balls and roll in fine coconut. (I used home-grown corn ground in a seed grinder.) I pressed the mixture firmly into a melon ball scoop—makes 30 flattened balls.
Variation: Add chopped raisins, dates or carob chips.

Tofu Candy (Prize Winner)

1 cup tofu,* mashed	1 tsp. vanilla
1 cup fine coconut	¼ tsp. salt
4 Tbsp. honey	½ cup dry milk (approx.)

Mix the first five ingredients, adding enough dry milk powder to make it manageable and roll into balls.

* See Homemade Food Items, page 160.

Potato Candy (Delicious)

2 cups mashed potatoes	1 tsp. vanilla
1 cup medium coconut	pinch salt

¼ cup chopped dates
2 Tbsp. carob
4 Tbsp. honey

1/8 tsp. ginger
2 cups dry milk (or more)

Hint: If you do not have coconut or dates, do this: Mix the potato, dry milk, carob and honey. Roll out in ¼ inch roll and spread with peanut butter and jam. Serve in small strips.

Variation: 2 drops oil of peppermint flavoring (purchase at the pharmacy) and walnuts in place of dates. Form into balls and roll in fine coconut. Refrigerate.

Desserts Using Dried Fruits, Grains, Nuts and Vegetables

No Meat Mince Pie

1 cup raisins
2 cups dried fruit, soaked
   and ground (apples,
   prunes or other fruit)

2 cups ground gluten,
   (beef flavored)
1 cup fruit juice thick-
   ened with 2 Tbsp. arrowroot

Mix all together and add ½ cup honey, 1 Tbsp. lemon juice and 2 Tbsp. oil. Add: ½ tsp. each allspice, cinnamon, cloves, nutmeg and salt. Bake in a crust or serve as a pudding; especially good warm.

Try a Quick Barley Pudding

Grind ¼ cup barley in a seed grinder. Add: 1 cup water, 1 egg, 1 Tbsp. honey. Add vanilla, cinnamon, lemon juice and salt to taste. Mix and strain through a fine strainer and cook until thick. Add raisins.

Potato Pudding

¼ cup each: potato
   starch, dry milk, carob
⅓ cup raw sugar

1/8 tsp. salt
2 Tbsp. butter or oil
½ tsp. vanilla

Combine in a blender with 1½ cups boiling water. This makes an instant good pudding. It can be thickened more by cooking in a double boiler. I make my own potato starch and pre-mix the dry ingredients (to use as I would a package pudding).

Parsnip Pudding—Surprisingly good

2 cups mashed, strained parsnips	½ cup cream
	¼ tsp. salt
3 Tbsp. honey	½ tsp. vanilla

Blend until smooth. Carob, nuts, orange juice, or rind could be added.

Cauliflower Cream

Tiny pieces of raw cauliflower with slices of banana in whipped cream.

Frozen Bananas

Dip ripe bananas in carob syrup, roll in coconut or nuts. Freeze in separate plastic bags.

Carob Syrup

½ cup carob powder	½ cup honey
⅓ cup milk	2 tsp. vanilla

Cook five minutes.

Homemade Food Items

Tofu

Tofu (pronounced "toe-foo") is a soy cheese known as boneless meat, used in Oriental cooking. It has been a staple in China for over 2,000 years.

It has several advantages:

—It can be combined with more expensive or scarce animal proteins (eggs, cheese, meat, fish or nut butters).

—It has almost no flavor when mixed with these other foods. It takes on their flavor.

—It contains 35 grams of protein per pound and yet has less than half the calories per gram of usable protein in a lamb chop, for example.

—One pound of dry soybeans (2½ cups) will make more than 1½ pounds of soy cheese.

—Unlike meat it has no cholesterol. One report asserts that a man with a heart condition greatly improved with the use of tofu as protein every day.

Learning how tofu was made commercially here in Portland, helped me get the process straight in my mind and made the job easier in my own kitchen. The object is:

—To grind the soaked beans to get some soy milk; strain.
—Then boil the milk and curdle it.
—Drain off the whey and have a ball of cheese. (Like making cottage cheese).

Making the Soy Milk—for Tofu

—Soak 3 cups of dry soybeans for about 6 hours.
—Blend 1 cup of the soaked beans at a time in a blender with 3 cups of water.
—Strain out the residue, using a clean cloth. (There will be ways to use it, but it is the milk you want for the cheese.)
—Put another 3 cups of water and 1 cup of beans in the blender until they are all liquified.
—Add enough boiling water to the strained milk to make 6 quarts.

Curdling the Milk

—Bring milk to boiling point. Boil for 3 minutes and remove from heat. (Use a large pan as it boils over easily.)*
—Add ½ tsp. citric acid,** dissolved in ¼ cup of hot water. Stir gently only a time or two. (Buy citric acid at drug store.)
—Cover and let stand for 5 to 10 minutes.
—Gently lift the curd into a colander lined with cheesecloth. Sprinkle 1 tsp. of salt over cheese if desired.

* To eliminate such close watching and stirring to prevent sticking to the bottom of the pan, I heat the milk in a double boiler (or a smaller pan inside a larger pan) until it reaches the boiling point and then put directly on the heat to bring to a rolling boil.

** Some use a rounded teaspoon of citric acid. But ½ tsp. coagulates the milk. Or use lemon juice or 2 Tbsp. epsom salts dissolved in ¼ cup of water.

Draining and Molding the Curd

—Commercial tofu is handled very gently from here on. The end product is very soft, light and fragile yet it can be sliced or cubed.

—The curd is poured into a cheesecloth-lined box that has no top or bottom. The ends of the cloth are folded over the cheese.

—Most of the whey drains off.

—As pressure is applied from the top, remaining whey is forced out and the moisture on top is blotted up by using a dry piece of folded cheesecloth under the weight.

—Commercially the cheese is now cut into blocks and slid off the pallet into a tank of cool water. (At home slide it off into a jar filled with water.) It will keep for several days without refrigeration by changing the water a few times a day to keep an even cool temperature.

To the Orientals, cheese making is an art. I stood for hours and watched their flowing graceful motions as they handled their cheese. While repeating the process in my own kitchen with my husband, before we mastered the art, the scene was anything but peaceful—with milk that boiled all over the stove, scorched pans to clean, blenders and pans and cloths to wash, floors, cupboards, curtains, walls and windows splattered with milk and whey, and residue to use or waste.

But I promise you with a little patience, you can make good cheese with a minimum of effort.

Simple Tofu Recipe

1. Blend 1 cup raw, dry soybeans in blender (or use soaked soybeans and grind some other way).

2. Add to 6 cups boiling water. Stir to dissolve lumps.

3. Boil 3 to 5 minutes. Remove from stove and add ½ cup cold water.

4. Add 3 Tbsp. vinegar or lemon juice (or other curdling agent).

5. Stir gently until it curdles.
6. Strain through colander lined with cloth.
7. Discard the whey (or use in bread making) or drink it.
8. Gather up edges of cloth and twist to squeeze out liquid.
9. Use crumbly cheese to extend tuna fish, hamburger or scrambled eggs.

Learning to make gluten wasn't easy either. See *Passport to Survival,* page 38. A simplified method is to eliminate the pounding. Try this: Soak 7 cups flour and 6 cups water for ½ hour or more. Wash out the starch, use in gluten recipes.

Gluten Sausages [1]

2 cups ground, baked gluten   2 Tbsp. olive oil
2 eggs   2 tsp. sausage seasoning*
2 Tbsp. whole wheat flour

Mix and mold into desired shape. Bake at 350° for 20 minutes. Then fry in bacon grease or olive oil. Serve hot. Try not to get them too tough or dry. Variation: In place of baked gluten, soak cracked wheat, wash out starch, air dry an hour or so (watch long elastic threads develop).

* For seasoning, see Homemade Food Items, p. 222.

Gluten Parmesan Cheese Steaklets

Melt 3 Tbsp. butter in a square baking dish. Dip about 24 small gluten steaklets in canned milk. Roll in 2 Tbsp. Parmesan cheese mixed with ¼ cup flour. Put in pan and bake 20 minutes at 350°. Mix ⅓ cup canned milk with ½ cup Parmesan cheese and let stand. Pour a can of tomato sauce around steaklets. Spread cheese mixture over top and bake 20 to 30 minutes at 350°.

Gluten Patties

Two cups each ground cooked gluten and rice. Add 1 egg and 1 onion (finely chopped). Season with 3 Tbsp. soy sauce, ½ tsp. sage, ¼ tsp. garlic salt. Add 1 Tbsp. flour if necessary to hold the patties together. Bake covered for 30 minutes at 350°. Serve with tomato sauce if desired.

Pickling and Relishes

Try pickled raw fish!
—Leave the fish in the salt for a week.

----

1. LeArta Moulton, "The Gluten Book."

—Skin and cut in bite-size pieces and soak in fresh water to remove the salt.

—Pack in glass jars and cover with a pickling solution made from:

6 cups water, 2 quarts vinegar (5%), ½ cup honey, 1 Tbsp. salt, ¼ cup pickling spice, 2 medium onions in rings (garlic, optional)

This makes a gallon of pickling solution. The pickled fish will keep well under refrigeration for about 6 months. Allow a week or so for the bones to soften before using.

Easy Dill Pickles

If you want to pickle a few surplus cucumbers from a small garden, it is convenient to have a gallon of pickling brine ready. Every few days as your cucumbers ripen, pack them in sterile jars. Heat sufficient brine to the boiling point and pour the liquid over the cucumbers to within ½ inch of the top. Seal the jars and that is all you do.

Two brine recipes for dill pickles:
—Mix 3 quarts water, 1 quart white vinegar, 7/8 cup non-iodized salt and sprigs of dill.

You may prefer a pickling solution using less salt but more vinegar. For a small amount use:
—2 cups water, 1 cup vinegar, 1 Tbsp. non-iodized salt and a sprig of dill.

Other spices can be added, but are not necessary:

Mustard seed	Whole pickling spice
Whole peppercorns	Pieces of fresh horseradish
Bay leaves	Grape leaves

Grape leaves added to pickles are said to make the pickles crisp like alum does.

Korean Chow

Fill a gallon jar with sliced:

Red and green cabbage	Young mustard greens
Cauliflower	A little garlic and
Radishes with tops	Hot red pepper

—Add 1 or 2 Tbsp. of salt and cover with water.
—Stand at room temperature for 2 days.
—Keep vegetables under the liquid.

—Store in the refrigerator. It will be ready to eat in 3 or 4 days.

Vegetable Juice Cocktail

Use ⅔ tomato juice and ⅓ other vegetable juices such as onion, parsley, pepper, celery and carrot.

Vinegar

Apple Cider Vinegar — Vinegar can be made from apples, peaches, pears, honey or grapes (which make a beautiful blue vinegar).

Homemade vinegar, kefir, tofu, pudding. Top to bottom: apples, juice, the mother, vinegar acidophilus, milk, kefir, soy beans, soy milk, tofu, potatoes, starch, pudding.

Step One

—1 bushel of apples makes 2 to 3 gallons of juice. Use a juicer or cider press.
—Let the juice stand at room temperature for a day or two in any glass, wood or stone jar that has been scalded well.

—Pour into a clean container leaving the sediment at the bottom.

Step Two

—Add 1 yeast cake dissolved in water for every 4 gallons of juice. (Some recipes do not call for the yeast. I used it and was very pleased with the whole experiment. The vinegar was good.)
—Cover with layers of cheesecloth. It needs a dark even temperature.
—Stir every day for four or more days.

Step Three

—Empty again into a clean, scalded crock or bottle.
—To 4 parts of the apple juice, add 1 part old vinegar. (Buy it the first year; after that you will have a "mother" to start the next batch.)
—Exclude light but not air for 3 to 6 months. Temperature is best at 70°.
—Do not disturb the slippery gelatinous film. This is the "mother."
—Pour through flannel cloth wrung out in cold water. Bottle and cork tightly. Age for 6 months to a year.

Homemade Kefir

Kefir is a growing, living, fermented milk culture. It is a "yogurt" that you drink rather than eat with a spoon. The culture to sour the milk is sold in many forms. The Kefir "grains" I have resemble rubbery cottage cheese curds.

A friend who gave me a start bought hers 25 years ago in Mexico for $10 or so an ounce. When her family went to Europe for the summer, they took their "kernels" with them.

—Put kernels in milk and allow to stand at room temperature.
—The milk will coagulate in a day or so.
—The mixture of kernels and thick milk is passed through a sieve.
—The kernels are then washed off and covered with more milk or stored in water in the refrigerator.
—Kefir grows and multiplies only when it has milk to feed on. Keep the Kefir start growing like a sourdough yeast

start. You have to buy it only once (and will have plenty to share with your friends).

Some know the Kefir as lactobacillus acidophilus, a lactic acid bacteria that grows and multiplies and bubbles and ferments like yeast. The intestines of newborn babies are invaded by this "friendly bacteria." As we get older, these bacteria may be lacking and can be reintroduced into the intestines by using this culture.

The main reason for using Kefir is to aid elimination and also help the body synthesize important vitamins and retard the growth of harmful bacteria. It is also a way to keep milk without refrigeration and a way to greatly increase the value of reconstituted dry milk.

Most of the milk we have used for the past six years has been in this form. (Our favorite drink is frozen or fresh raspberries and the Kefir blended with a little honey.)

I am continuing my research on fermented foods. Kefir grains are obtainable in many health food stores and can be ordered by writing to R.A.J. Biological Laboratory, 35 Park Avenue, Blue Point, Long Island, New York.

Sandwich Fillings

The aim of this recipe section is to help families have tasty nutritious food, even under emergency situations. It is not easy to sift through my collection of recipes and not use those calling for ingredients that we may not have (like the green pepper sandwich filling I like that calls for cream cheese, olives, walnuts, lemons, butter, mayonnaise, etc.). What guarantee do we have that these will be on our kitchen shelves? We may be very thankful just to be able to sit down to a piece of bread and butter and crisp green pepper. Hopefully, we all will have legumes in our stored food supply. A puree made from soybeans, kidney beans, lima beans, peas or garbanzos make a good base for a sandwich filling.

Soak, cook, drain and mash the beans or peas (or put through a food press or grinder). Season to taste with salt, onions, pickle relish, and moisten with catsup or mayonnaise. After spreading one side of the bread with puree, add any of the following: chopped raw cabbage, water cress or carrots, green pepper, onion rings, tomato slices, chopped cooked beets, raw apple slices, dandelion or sour dock greens or nasturtium leaves or alfalfa sprouts. Add cheese, nuts, eggs or meat—if you are lucky enough to have some. (Try grated sharp cheese, cottage cheese, cream cheese, chopped peanuts or walnuts.) Two favorites are: (1) broiled bean sandwiches: toast one side of bread under broiler; then spread baked beans on untoasted side. Top with tomato and bacon and return to broiler for a few minutes until bacon is crisp and beans are heated through. (2) Tuna fish sandwiches with crisp, raw sprouted lentils instead of lettuce. Gluten ground, well seasoned, and spread on sandwiches with chopped parsley, onion and mayonnaise, is delicious. Just plain alfalfa sprouts and gluten with mayonnaise is good.

Peanut butter is an American favorite—try adding sliced banana or a slice of sweet raw onion (it is good) or wheat germ or brewers yeast mixed with peanut butter. Another favorite is honey and peanut butter (comb honey is good). Dried fruit and nuts make good sweet fillings for either open faced or plain sandwiches. In South America, they add dates to the soybean puree used on sandwiches. Try dates, walnuts and grated carrot together. Dried apples, dates, raisins, bananas and sunflower seeds all ground together are good. Wheat germ could be added (or any dried fruit you have). Ground fresh apple, added just before using, is good to moisten heavy fruit paste.

Spreads, Toppings and Fillings

Honey Fruit Spread

Juice from one lemon	1 cup sunflower seeds
1 cup honey	1 cup sesame seed
1 cup currants	1 cup soaked prunes

Tofu Icing

Add creamed tofu, drained crushed pineapple with enough dry milk to make it the right consistency. Blend in a blender. Add vanilla.

Sprouted Wheat Filling

Try sprouted wheat and coconut steamed in canned milk. Grind in Champion Juicer with the screen on. Add carob, peanut butter, lemon juice, honey, dry milk, mint flavor, vanilla and salt.

Whipped Topping

½ cup water   2 Tbsp. sugar
1 Tbsp. lemon juice   ¼ tsp. vanilla
½ cup dry milk

Sprinkle dry milk on water. Beat until stiff enough to stand in soft peaks. Add lemon juice and continue beating until stiff. Beat in sugar; add vanilla and chill.

Sweet Fillings

Extracting the sugar from vegetables was the only sweetening the pioneers had before 1852, according to one account. Honey, molasses and dried fruits were not available and, of course, sugar was not even manufactured then.

In desperation, they learned to boil down the beets, squash and carrots. The result was a gummy substance that they used for sweetening. They also found a sweetener by cutting a hole in the top of a ripe pumpkin, taking out the seeds and membrane through the hole and setting it outside for several frosty nights. A liquid would rise inside of the pumpkin which was boiled until syrupy and sweet. Sorghum cane was planted, the juice pressed out of the stalks and boiled down to a syrup. Syrup was also made from corn. Try:
- Mix honey and molasses with equal parts. Thin with a little water. Add maple, vanilla or butter flavoring. Use over hot cakes.
- Mix equal parts of fruit juice (raspberry juice), honey and thicken with arrowroot. (1 cup juice, 1 cup honey and ¼ cup arrowroot)
- Pears (ripe)—liquified, lemon and honey simmered makes good pear honey.
- Fresh red clover blossoms are very sweet. Make a concentrated tea, strain, thicken to honey consistency and combine in equal amounts with honey for a honey extender—good!

Seasonings Make a Difference

Vegetables do not always need seasoning, especially with the trend to more raw and less cooked ones. For a flavor change try these seasonings:

Beets — cloves, dill, allspice or bay leaves
Broccoli — caraway, rosemary, dill
Carrots — thyme, sesame seed, poppy seed, cloves
Cauliflower — celery seed, paprika, nutmeg
Corn — cayenne, chili powder, oregano
Green Beans — sesame seed, dill, marjoram, chili powder, chives
Lima Beans — sage, curry powder, nutmeg, chili powder
Mustard Greens — oregano
Onions — sage, thyme, oregano
Potatoes — celery seed, chives, mustard, paprika
Turnip Greens — oregano
Zucchini — bay leaves, dill marjoram, poppy seed, sage.

Use fresh herbs whenever you can, but remember three to four times as much fresh herbs are needed as dried ones.

Sauces, Dips, Dressings, Gravy

Uncooked Garbanzo Sauce

1 cup dry garbanzos   salt to taste
¼ cup lemon juice

Soak garbanzos overnight in about three cups of water. Add lemon juice and blend in an electric blender with a small amount of water. Season to taste. Serve cold over salads or hot over vegetables. (Combines well with mushroom soup over cooked wheat.)

Carrot Cream

¼ cup almond butter   ½ tsp. kelp or salt
  (try peanut butter)   2 cups carrot juice

Blend to a cream.

Cucumber Sauce

Blend cucumber, skin and all in a small amount of water. Thicken with avocado. Add lemon juice and seasoning. Serve as a dip for sliced cucumbers.

Horseradish Dressing

¼ cup fresh grated
  horseradish
¼ cup lemon juice

3 Tbsp. whole wheat flour
1 tsp. salt
1 ¼ cup hot water

Slowly add hot water to all ingredients except horseradish and thyme. Stir until boiling point is reached; remove from fire and add horseradish and thyme.

To make plain horesradish sauce:

Wash, peel, grate or grind the roots (that look like parsnips). Add only enough distilled vinegar to moisten the horseradish. (Cider vinegar causes horseradish to turn dark.) This keeps for several weeks in the refrigerator.

Frozen Horseradish Cream

Whip ¾ cup heavy cream until stiff. Add 1 Tbsp. prepared horseradish and 2 tsp. sugar and freeze until firm. Serve cold.

Frozen Vegetable Relish

Finely chop:
  3 sticks celery
  1 large green pepper
  1 large onion

3 large tomatoes, peeled
⅓ lb. mushrooms

Add:
  ½ cup catsup
  ½ tsp. marjoram

½ tsp. sweet basil
½ tsp. seasoned salt

This relish is delicious raw on hot dogs.

Pineapple Buttermilk Dressing (no oil)

Combine and bring to a boil:
  1 egg
  1 Tbsp. cornstarch
  ¼ tsp. salt

¼ tsp. paprika
1 8½ oz. can crushed
  pineapple

Blend in:
  1 tsp. prepared mustard
  1 cup buttermilk

1 Tbsp. lemon juice

This dressing is good with carrots, cabbage, Waldorf salad or any fruit combination.

Tofu Dressing*

1 cup tofu   ½ tsp. vegetable salt
¼ cup water   1 tsp. onion powder
2 Tbsp. lemon juice

Blend in blender.

* See Homemade Food Items, page 160.

French Salad Dressing

½ cup salad oil   1 tsp. paprika
⅓ cup vinegar   ½ tsp. salt
⅓ cup catsup   juice of ½ lemon
¼ cup honey   ½ medium onion, grated

Mix together. Shake well prior to using.

Lentil Gravy

1 cup mashed lentils   1 tsp. flour
½ cup water   seasoning
¼ cup chopped onion

Simmer gently and strain. Thicken with flour. Season with garlic or onion salt.

Note: With our small seed mills, many legumes can be ground and the fine meal sifted into hot soup stock. A good gravy can be made.

Brown Gravy with No Meat

For brown gravy when no meat is available, try using any of the following:
Toastum (dark parched ground wheat)
Instant Postum
Browned whole wheat flour
Parched dandelion root
Soy sauce (if it does not have MSG in it)
Commercial Gravy Master or Kitchen Bouquet

Nut Gravy

Use any nut butter, liquid, onion, garlic, tomatoes, bay leaf. Save it.

Note: Always use potato water or any vegetable juice in gravy.

Mayonnaise—no eggs or cooking

1 cup oil
½ cup milk, evaporated
1 tsp. honey
½ tsp. salt
¼ tsp. paprika

2 to 4 Tbsp. lemon juice
1 cup oil
2 more Tbsp. canned milk
½ tsp. prepared mustard

Oil, milk, bowl and beaters should be very cold. Measure honey, salt, paprika and ½ cup milk in bowl and beat well. Add ¼ cup oil, a drop or two at a time, and then the remainder of the oil and lemon juice alternately. Beat. Add the 2 Tbsp. milk and beat again. Good with potato salad.

Chapter 14

Frugal Ways With Food

Eating More Edible Parts of Plants

Finding More Food in the Garden

FOOD HAS BEEN SO PLENTIFUL IN AMERICA that we are in the habit of eating only certain parts of our fresh produce and throwing the rest away. It has been estimated that if we ate the produce in its entirety—leaves, stems, roots and seeds—we could feed more than ten times our current population.

Consider using the following foods without any waste. You will find additional benefits of meal variations.

Radish — Eat the radish and the top as well, or use the top in a green drink. Tiny crisp seed pods in salads taste like the radish itself. (They go to seed the first year.)

Cauliflower and cabbage — Use the outer leaves. Liquify, strain, add to cream sauce. Dice the core and eat cooked or raw.

Broccoli leaves and stems — If tough, peel the stem and steam.

Garlic and leek — The root and the blossom taste just like the clove itself. Wash, dry and powder.

Peppers — If you want to add bioflavonoids (Vitamin C complex), use the white part and the seeds.

Pumpkins and squash — Scoop out seeds and membrane, blend, strain and add soup stock and seasoning for a nutritious soup. Roots and young leaves are used in stew. The male zucchini flower (not the one that has the zucchini on it) is good baked with a meat loaf stuffing.

Peas — Liquify fresh pea pods in a blender, strain and add to cream soup. Dry the pods and powder for soup. The leaves are good in green drinks.

Corn — Early settlers used every part:

—Young plants thinned out (suckers) were boiled as greens.

—Three-foot stalks were roasted on ashes and eaten, before the ears began to form.

—When silk appeared, ears were chopped up and boiled to make a kind of soup. The silk was used for tea.

—When kernels formed, they were scraped off, mashed and boiled.

—When the ears were full and ripe, they were enjoyed to the fullest.

—Older corn with hard kernels was ground and worked with the hands to form a stiff dough. It was placed in husks and baked in ashes or poured out on hot cooking rocks to make piki or paper bread.

—In times of famine, corn cobs were dried, ground and used for flour. Husks were fed to horses and cattle.

Beans — Try eating them from the time the bean pods first form until they mature. Pods can be roasted, ground and used like cornmeal. The vines can be dried and ground into meal to give dark color to bread.

Spinach — Instead of cutting off the spinach, pull the whole plant and use it all for a tremendous saving in nutrients.

Parsnip — Eat the root, the stalk (like celery) and the green leaves.

Sweet Potato — Leaves make delicious greens.[1]

Lettuce — If it grows too tall and is bitter at the top, use the lower leaves that are tender and sweet.

Cabbage — A root left in the ground last fall sprouted six new small heads this spring.

Potatoes — Make potato starch from the culls and use for smooth puddings or with whole wheat flour for cakes.

Alfalfa — The nodules under the plants are good to eat.

Mint — Recently, at a fund raising dinner, we served mint tea from the garden to 110 people. (At the store it costs 85 cents for about 1½ ounces.)

Basil — My neighbor planted a packet of basil seed and cut the pretty green leaves just before they were in full bloom. She

---

1. "Organic Method Primer," page 153.

now has two quarts of dried basil. It is her favorite seasoning for tomato and vegetable dishes.

Neighborhood Dill Crock — In the fall, the last few stray vegetables could be gathered up and combined to make a big dill crock to be divided later.

Cores, Seeds, Pits and Peelings from Fruit — Apple tea made from dried trimmings of apples using core, seeds, peel and all is a favorite South American beverage.

- —Soak peelings from fruit overnight in water and strain. It makes a good drink.
- —Dried pear cores are surprisingly good.
- —Dried apples (seeds, skin and all) ground fine are good.
- —I poured prune puree over the prune kernels and dried in the dehydrator.
- —Grapefruit seeds contain oil that can be used in making salad dressing.
- —Dry orange and lemon peel and powder for flavoring.
- —Scrape the underside of a banana skin and dry it. (Very sweet.)
- —Eat the inside of thick skinned oranges. (Low in calories.)
- —Make cantaloupe seed milk in a blender or dry and parch them. Do the same with watermelon seed. Peach, apricot, cherry and prune pits are good to eat. (Apricot pits have cobalt in them.)

Using Abundant Crops

Most countries have one or more abundant food crops. Where coconut is plentiful, it is used in countless ways. In this country, maybe we have a surplus of apples, pears, carrots, beans and potatoes that are going to waste.

Ways to Use Carrots

Listing ways to use carrots may stimulate our thinking about ways to use other plentiful foods.

- —Carrot Juice: serve plain or with milk. Make ice cream popsicles, or boil down to a sweet syrup.
- —Use the pulp in cookies, crackers or cake.
- —Raw carrots can be cut into sticks, curls or in cookie cutter shapes.
- —Grate carrots in cookies, cakes, puddings, muffins, crackers or bread.

—Cooked carrots are good in cream soup and stews, mashed with potatoes, in a loaf with eggs, cheese and rice, candied like sweet potatoes, baked, cubed, slivered and sliced.

—Carrots can be dried in paper thin chips; dried and powdered for broth.

—Carrots grated fine and dried keep their color and are fresh tasting for a salad. Rehydrate with pineapple juice or water, or just eat dry for a snack.

—Carrots grated, dried, ground and then browned make a good coffee substitute.

—Carrots can be pickled in vinegar or bottled for soup.

—Carrot Tops: Add a few tops when making juice. Lay a handful of clean tops over carrots you are steaming (some of the food value will seep in). Have some fresh tender greens for salads by planting the crown of the carrot in a container of damp sand or in a dish of water. (Leave about a half inch of the stems on the crown.)

Note: Grow other greens the same way from turnips, parsnips or beets. String beans, like carrots, can be used in many

Green beans can be used in many different ways.

ways such as fresh, frozen, bottled, dried, fermented, or left on the vine to mature and shell for dry beans.

Free Food for the Gathering

We are surrounded with nourishing edible plants and should take advantage of this free food growing in our yards or nearby fields and mountains. It is up to each individual to search out what is edible in his locality.

In the Northwest the plants I am the most familiar with are:

Flowers — Books on edible flowers tell about salads from tender leaves and flowers of pansies, violets and marigolds. There are recipes for nasturtiums in mayonnaise, dandelion petals in cream sauce, hollyhocks, day lilies and purple milkweed flowers in soup. Tea from elderberries or orange blossoms is good. Orange and lemon peel are used for flavoring. Marigolds are ground for flour. Day lily buds are a delicacy.

Edible flowers—dried marigolds, dandelion greens, mallow leaves and seeds, sour dock, nasturtiums, violets.

Fruits

—Elderberries, fresh or dried, contain Vitamin C.
—Wild Blackberries (last summer I picked 18 gallons)—
   freeze whole, make juice, combine with other juices,
   puree and make fruit leather or dry as currants.
—Huckleberries—A friend tells of her mother bottling 150
   quarts on a camp stove in a copper boiler while the family
   was on vacation.
—Rose Hips[1] —One mother had 35 pounds of rose hips in
   her deep freeze. They can be dried on strings and crushed
   as needed for herb tea.
—Wild grape and Oregon grape have tasty fruit. The purple
   berries make good juice.

Note: Recently, a friend sent me a booklet on using flowers to make a "Rescue Remedy" (a first-aid or emergency remedy). It is used for reducing feelings of terror, shock, mental tension, and loss of emotional control. She wants to carry a bottle of the tincture in her purse in case of even an automobile accident. All inquiries should be addressed to:

   The Secretary, The Dr. Edward Bach Centre
   Mount Vernon, Sotwell, Wallingford,
   Berkshire, OX10 OPZ

Beverages — Dandelion root, scrubbed and roasted about four hours, then ground, makes a good dark drink. Chicory root, prepared as the dandelion root, is an excellent substitute for coffee. Needles of the Douglas Fir make a good herb tea. Also use wild mint, stinging nettle, leaves and roots of wild Oregon grape and leaves of wild black currant.

Salad Greens — Use very young leaves of burdock, clover, chicory, dandelion, wild onion, shepherd's purse, sour dock.

Vegetable substitute — Try these substitutes in place of the commonly-used vegetables:

Burdock Root — Slice diagonally and simmer 1 to 2 hours with onions, lentils and barley.

Thistle Stems — Peel and boil.

Blackberry Shoots — Peel in spring before the thorns harden and cook the young tender shoots.

---

1. Rose hips are the fruit of the rose and are filled with seeds. After the petals fall off and the first frost comes, they are ready to harvest.

Fern — Remove the fiddle back (curled up top) and eat the tender stem below it.

Tumbleweed — Eat the bright green shoots that break off easily. (This plant has great resistance to drought.)

Mustard Flower Buds — Cook 3 minutes.

Cooked Greens — Lambs' quarters, mustard, purslane, dandelion, malva, sheep sorrel (or 'sour dock' vinegar plant) and stinging nettle (collect when less than 1 foot tall) contain vitamins A, C and protein.

Dried herb teas: yarrow, camomile, sage, brigham, alfalfa, mint, raspberry, comfrey.

Chickweed — The small fresh green leaves of this prolific plant can be picked in early spring and frozen or dried for winter.

Cattails — Cook the whitish roots like asparagus. They grow horizontally out from the main root, about two inches long. The roots are full of starch that can be baked or made into a sticky dough. Wash and peel roots, put in clean water, break, mash, shake and soak. The starch will dissolve into the water and settle to the bottom. Let stand overnight and pour off clear water and use in biscuits and such.

Milkweed Flower Buds — (Unopened with tiny stems and pods.) Blanch for one minute in three different baths of boiling water. Serve in cream sauce with grated cheese.

Flour — There are 300 varieties of grasses that produce seeds and grains that can be ground into flour. Seeds from knotgrass and lambs quarters are examples. Cattail pollen, used with equal parts of wheat flour, makes yellow pancakes and muffins. They are good! I have tried them.

Poisonous Plants

Be careful not to use plants that are poisonous, such as the following:

Flowers and Bulbs: Poinsettia, certain lilies, hyacinth bulbs, daffodil bulbs, jasmine, oleander, azalias.

Shrubs, Trees: Some varieties of sumac, hemlock, caster beans and seeds, green berries, foliage of black nightshade, mistletoe berries, peach leaves,[1] apple seeds.[2]

Vegetables: Potato leaves, eyes, sprouts of green potatoes, tomato leaves.

Other Plants: Rhubarb leaves, chokecherries, horsechestnut, pokeweed roots; shoots, leaves and bark of elderberry.

Note: Euell Gibbons said, "I don't know of a flowering plant that tastes good and is poisonous. Nature is not out to get you." *Parade Magazine,* January 30, 1972. However, we should make sure plants are edible before trying them.

Food Substitutes in the Kitchen

Great satisfaction is derived from making foods from natural sources, and at the same time reducing the usual lengthy grocery list for the supermarket.

Honey Substitutes and Extenders

Extracting natural sugars from plants, fruits and vegetables can be a fun family experiment.

Red-Clover Honey — Get some honey where the bees get theirs. Gather a bucket of red clover blossoms and make a strong tea. Thicken with arrowroot or cornstarch (3 Tbsp. to a cup of tea). Mix one cup of thick tea with one cup honey. If you do not have

---

1. People have used peach leaf tea with no ill effects. Perhaps other plants listed are toxic, but not deadly poisonous.

2. About apple seeds: When quantities of 50 or more seeds are chewed, they produce cyanide complex in the blood and can be fatal. ("Common Poisonous Plants in Home and Grounds," Extension Service Bulletin No. 466A, Colorado State University, page 17.)

clover blossoms, add thickened fruit juice to the honey. For variety, add flavorings and cake coloring.

Fruit Concentrates — This fall we made ten special trays for the dehydrator with ¾ inch sides. In them we poured 6 gallons of apple cider and evaporated it down to one gallon of thick syrup. Delicious! A local bakery uses thick concentrates from dates, prunes, raisins and figs.

Sugar Beets, Corn, Carrots, Pumpkin, Pears, Melons — Before sugar factories, pioneers boiled down the beets to a gummy consistency to use as sweetening. It works! In California one fall, oversized beets and carrots from the garden (juiced in the juicer) were boiled down to make a sweet syrup.

When freezing or drying corn, extract the sweet juice from corn cobs. Cover the cobs with water and boil. Remove cobs, strain and boil down the juice.

For pumpkin syrup, pioneers did this: Cut a hole in top of a ripe pumpkin. Remove the seeds and stringy parts. Set the pumpkin outside for several frosty nights. A liquid will rise inside. Pour it off and save it. Boil until syrupy and sweet.

If a watermelon is rather mealy, juice or grind the rind, pulp, seeds and all. Boil it down to a sweet syrup. Do the same with mealy pears.

Molasses, Sorghum and Maple Trees — Mix honey with equal amounts of molasses. It is less expensive and higher in calcium and iron. (One tablespoon of blackstrap molasses has 137 mg. of calcium and 3.2 mg. iron. One tablespoon of strained honey has 1 mg. of calcium and 0.1 mg. iron. Light molasses has 33 mg. calcium per tablespoon.) [1]

I would like to plant some sorghum cane and make my own molasses—or plant sugar maple trees. The sap could drip into a bucket hanging on the tree and then be boiled down into syrup.

Fruit and Vegetable Substitutes

Picture a family on a cold winter night in Wyoming around the fire. They are studying or reading stories while eating sliced raw potatoes, cold and crisp, which the father brings up nightly from the cellar and peels for each one (in lieu of apples they don't have). Potatoes do not taste like apples, but this is a fond memory of my friend from Wyoming.

---

1. Bogert, Briggs & Calloway, "Nutrition and Physical Fitness," Philadelphia, W. B. Saunders Company, 1973, page 555-557.

—Sprouted rye could pass for expensive wild rice, or
—Jerusalem artichokes for water chestnuts when used in Chinese food.
—Parsnip pudding will surprise you. See page 160.

Milk Substitutes
(See Beverages in Chapter 13)

With our modern blenders, we can make liquids from various foods that have the appearance of milk. Try blending peanuts, cashews, almonds or fresh coconut, sesame seeds, cantalope seeds, sprouted unhulled millet, barley, wheat, or soybeans, using about one cup to a quart of water. Blend to a smooth consistency, strain and heat if desired. Flavor with carob, vanilla, a drop of lemon juice or other flavoring.

"Milkless Milk" with Eggs

For a quart of "milk," blend:
2 hard boiled eggs	¼ cup water
1 cup cooked brown rice	¼ cup honey (or less)

Blend, strain, chill and add enough more water to make a quart.

Whipped Powdered Milk — Whip 1 cup ice water and 1 cup non-instant powdered milk until thick. Add 1 tsp. lemon juice, sweeten to taste and flavor with vanilla.*

* "Natural Sweet Treats," by Laughlin, page 28.

Whipped Evaporated Milk — Pour milk in a refrigerator tray and chill until ice crystals begin to form. Beat until stiff. Add lemon juice and sweetening as desired.

Cream Substitute — Blend 1 cup ice water, ⅓ cup dry non-instant milk and 1 Tbsp. oil.

Butter — Dehydrated commercial shortening, water and coloring have been used as a butter substitute. Extend a pound of butter with liquid lecithin and oil or try adding one cup vegetable oil and whip for about five minutes; then refrigerate.

Soya Butter — Surprisingly good! Brown soy flower in the oven 1 hour at 200°. Mix with any vegetable oil. (Cold pressed safflower oil has amino acids not found in soybeans.)

Milk Curdling Agent — I sampled thistle cheese in Montana. The milk was curdled with thistle blossoms instead of rennet tablets. The purple blossom on globe artichokes can be used as well. The cheese was good with no objectionable flavor. To prepare the thistle, dry it for winter use, or if fresh, pick before thistle down begins to appear. Soak in a little water for five minutes. Pound, then repeat three times until a dark brown liquid forms. Strain and add five teaspoons to every gallon of warm milk you want curdled.

More Ways to Save

Leftovers

On baking day, plan on cleaning out your refrigerator. Flour is a natural vehicle to carry small amounts of leftover food.

Frig Cleaning Bread Recipe

On October 23, 1976, I was looking through the glass doors of my oven at nine loaves of bread. My silent prayer for success with my experiment was answered. The loaves raised well above the top of the pans and were later sliced thin, dried and packed in wide-mouth gallon jars and consumed by scouts, grandchildren, family and friends. The recipe included:

—Sour milk and cream, apple cider and lemon juice.

—Two eggs, a little butter, sesame seeds, honey and molasses.

—One banana, 2 persimmons, moist dried plums, and peaches.

—The usual yeast, salt and whole wheat flour.

—Other times, I might use a little cheese, avocado, rice, cereal or mayonnaise.

I find recipes in my files for cakes using carrots, potatoes (white or sweet), pumpkin, sauerkraut, zucchini, tomato soup, banana, apple, or dried fruit. (Of course, if you have a failure from using these things, slice the soggy loaf and dry it out for crackers and crumbs.

Don't Spill It!

Maybe in the future when food is scarce, we will be thankful for the habit of being careful and preventing waste.
—When buying in bulk there is much pouring and repackaging to be done. The wheat, seeds, legumes and other grains, dry milk, honey and many other items are poured from one container to another. A fruit filler or small funnel helps. Keep scoops or measuring cups in containers of grains and legumes.

Grind Your Own and Save

One family who normally purchased all their bakery goods, invested in a home grain mill. They saved $200 in one year, besides giving the family better quality food. You can grind:
Wheat for bread; rice for cakes.
—Whole dry peas for soup at a fraction of the cost of a can or packet.
—Soy flour, barley, oats, rye, lentils, beans and carob beans. (Carob beans grind into a fine powder which resembles chocolate in flavor and color. It has nutritional value worthy of our consideration—Vitamin A, thiamin, riboflavin, and the important minerals. It has high pectin content and is a natural protection against diarrhea.)
With all these various grits, grinds and flours, you have a whole new experience in food preparation awaiting you.

Shop Wisely

Families that buy together, save together—whether it is a 60 pound cheese block or a bag of mung beans to be divided.

Drying Food — Waste Not, Want Not!

Since the human body requires balanced nutrition, and since fresh fruits and vegetables may not always be available, then dried, canned, or frozen products are necessary. In war-torn Europe, following World War II, malnutrition was probably due more to the lack of fruits than to any other one thing.

Economies of Drying

Storage Space — Dried foods take one-tenth or less the storage space of wet pack. For example, half a bushel of apricots dried can be stored in two quart jars and one pint jar. About 100 pounds of tomatoes dried and powdered will fill a gallon jar.

Bottles and lids have been in short supply some seasons. Homemakers have found that many of the lids would not seal, resulting in waste and frustration.

Dry the surplus — A home garden and fruit trees can supply a large proportion of a family's produce needs. The trouble is, harvest brings too much all at once, and after the bottles and shelves are filled with full bottles, what do you do? Dry it!

Dri-best food dehydrator.

The fluctuating price of sugar forces us to reduce our consumption. Also, more and more researchers are discovering the detrimental effects of excessive sugar on the human body.

Energy is saved by drying, even if a dehydrator is used. An electric oven at its lowest setting uses very little electricity (about five cents per hour, which is also the average cost of an electric dehydrator).

Make your own convenience foods for really great savings:

Seasoning salts by blending dried onions, celery tops, garlic, etc.

Instant soup mix by combining dried vegetables in a blender.

Baby food by using small amounts of powdered vegetables and simmering till cooked, as well as rehydrating fruits.

Jerky made from game meat or beef.

Dip chips by slicing zucchini, potatoes, cucumbers, tomatoes, carrots and drying.

Sportsman's energy snacks — instead of candy for a quick-energy pickup, consider these more nutritional alternatives: dried fruits and fruit leathers, fruit balls, fruit flavored yogurt leather. One mother dried pork and beans for her backpackers, then chili, beef stew, chili sauce leather, rehydrated with boiling water; grated carrots rehydrated with pineapple juice.

In addition to fruits and vegetables, we can dry anything that has moisture in it: grasses, leaves, weeds, seeds, nuts, roots, meat, fish and foul.

Jars of fresh and dried tomatoes, butternut squash and corn, top-onions, chives, parsley, garlic, mushrooms, zucchini—sliced, dried and powdered.

Sweet Treats

Young mothers everywhere tell me the reason they started drying food was to provide sweet treats for their children instead of buying so many candies, cookies and ice creams. Most children prefer fruit leathers because they are more like candy. Store in bite-size pieces in a snack jar. (Your supply can soon be depleted if it is stored in rolls and your children share with their friends.) Pear pieces sprinkled with red jello look and taste like a confection; pear halves with a little of the pear center scooped out and filled with drained, crushed pineapple are delicious. Apple slices with cinnamon and sugar sprinkled on lightly is a favorite of many children.

My homemade Christmas gifts are usually blocks of dried fruit—a combination of ground fruits with seeds, nuts, and coconut added. Or I may send over to a neighbor a Christmas plate of dried fruit slices, fruit balls dipped in carob, centered with a heap of nuts. I enjoy sending missionaries a long roll of fruit leather, and have sent many samples to health missionaries for displays. Your imagination can provide an unlimited field of ideas for sweet treat creations, and family members will love to assist in the making.

Learning to Use a Dehydrator

I've seen experienced operators who sell dehydrators, dry food to perfection, but I guarantee they had a few failures in the learning process. The new books on dehydrating help to increase our skills. Some things I've learned from experience may be helpful:
— Black spots on tomatoes, peaches and apricots were caused from too cool a temperature. Overripe apricots turned dark in the center. Overdrying may also cause dark spots.
— The riper the fruit, the longer it will take to dry.
— A whole dehydrator full of sliced squash fermented because it was drying too slow in a garage where cold air was coming in the dehydrator.

What to do—

— Bring the dehydrator in from the outside if the temperature drops below 60 degrees.
— Overripe fruit should be started at a 10 degree higher temperature than normal. (Remember, fruit at its peak of ripeness brings best results.)
— For those concerned about vitamin loss from high heat, remember the temperature of the thermostat doesn't

indicate the temperature inside the pieces of fruit which could be about 35 degrees cooler.

—If the air is very humid, and juicy wet fruit is being dried, it will take a higher temperature to begin with; lower the temperature at the end of the drying period.

—Authorities agree—the faster you dry food, the less Vitamin C is lost. A new nitrogen pack sold is useful to remove oxygen. In storing, fill containers to the top and squeeze all the air out of plastic bags you are storing food in.

Preserving the Color and Texture

Antioxidants preserve color, vitamins and stop enzyme activity. Sometimes I use lemon juice, honey and water, ascorbic acid powder from the drug store or vitamin C tablets (six 500 mg. tablets crushed and dissolved in a cup of water).

The secret of preserving the color without using antioxidants is to work with great speed. Put one tray in at a time as fast as it is filled. Be sure the temperature is high enough, especially if you have a heavy load of juicy fruit.

If vegetables are to be rehydrated, they will be more tender if steamed first. (String beans are a superior product if steamed, frozen and then dried.) Onions, tomatoes, garlic, beets, herbs and mushrooms need no steaming. Grapes dry to raisins in less than one third the regular time if steamed first until they are transparent.

Test for Dryness

This comes with experience:

—Most dried fruits will have a flexible, leather, rubbery feel (like the lobe of your ear) with no juicy moist spots inside.

—Most vegetables should be dry and brittle; some are crisp or tough.

—Home dried fruit will be firmer than commercially dried fruit as anti-mold preservative has usually been added to the commercial product.

Storing — I store mine in bottles, but put some in the deep freeze if I don't think the fruit is dry enough. Another precaution against spoilage is:

—Cover jars with clean lids and screw bands loosely.

—Set fruit in a pre-heated 200 degree oven for 30 minutes.

—Remove jars from oven, tighten bands and cool.

Reconstituting

Vegetables: Soak, steam and serve. I use most dried vegetables in soup. Corn is delicious with cream sauce. Carrots grated
fine and dried, rehydrated in pineapple juice, make a tasty salad.
Cabbage rehydrates well. It is quick and easy to dry cut in half-
inch slices and spread out on trays.

Fruit: For hand to mouth eating or fruit leather, take no additional preparation (except for baby food).

—Soak and steam dried fruit slices for fruit soups.

—Moist breakfast fruit — cover with water, pour off immediately, stand overnight and serve.

Alternate Places to Dry Food Indoors and Out

Pilgrims, pioneers, Indians, explorers and soldiers on land
and sea have survived with dried foods in off-season. Without
modern dehydrators, where did they dry food? What can we im-
provise? It is interesting to learn that on top of Masada (which is
a mesa by the Dead Sea) were found edible dehydrated fruits—
raisins, dates, figs, and also grains. They were stored there for
King Herod, and were excavated by geologists in 1967.

Warm places in our home — Small amounts of food could be
dried in the following places:

—Heat registers in the floor. In cold weather dry thin sliced
apples in clean nylon tockings.

—Oven: One girl screwed a 100 watt light bulb in the oven,
put fiberglas mesh over the racks, kept the door propped
open with a lid and dried food continuously. Special racks
can be built to fit your oven.

—Suspend a small screen rack over the hot water heater,
radiator, electric heater, top of refrigerator, over the wood
burning stove, or in a south or west window.

—Hot attics — A friend tells of having small strips of meat
on a long line swaying in the breeze in their attic, with
open windows at either end.

Furnace rooms in public buildings — In a critical food crisis,
perhaps schools, churches and hospitals would permit food to be
dried on racks in their warm furnace rooms.

Bakery ovens — The owner of a small bakery told me he
could dry food for thousands of people. There is enough heat left
in the ovens after the day's baking to dry some foods. The temperature could be regulated if needed.

Drying outdoors — An antique dehydrator had a metal fire box under it. A small oil or wood burning stove could be used outside under drying racks. Build an open fire and dry fish or meat around the smouldering coals on lines or attached to boards as primitive man did.

In Thailand, I saw bananas drying on the south side of the house in big round shallow bowls with glass over the top. Match sticks were inserted under the glass to allow air passage.

Fruit leather mass-produced — In California, a family made quantities of fruit leather to send with their children going away to college. They covered big ping pong tables and a picnic table with sheets of plastic. One pitcher of apricot puree after another was poured on them. The sun did the rest.

Air dry on strings — A pretty way to dry food is to string such things as cranberries, cherries, figs, dates, grapes, persimmons, apple rings, strips of winter squash, colorful red peppers, or young tender string beans. Use a strong thread and a long needle and push through the center of whatever you are drying. Hang the decorative strings in a hot, shady place to air dry.

Heat from car window — One girl dried many racks of fruit inside her car. She faced the car to the south and slanted the rack from the steering wheel to the dashboard.

Instructions for dehydrating are covered in many new books.

Chapter 15

Cooking and Preserving Food

Cooking Grains, Beans and Other Foods

IF SHORT OF COOKING FUEL, make an "insulated nest."[1]

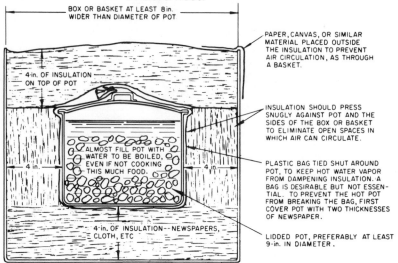

BOX OR BASKET AT LEAST 8 in. WIDER THAN DIAMETER OF POT

PAPER, CANVAS, OR SIMILAR MATERIAL PLACED OUTSIDE THE INSULATION TO PREVENT AIR CIRCULATION, AS THROUGH A BASKET.

4-in. OF INSULATION ON TOP OF POT

INSULATION SHOULD PRESS SNUGLY AGAINST POT AND THE SIDES OF THE BOX OR BASKET TO ELIMINATE OPEN SPACES IN WHICH AIR CAN CIRCULATE.

ALMOST FILL POT WITH WATER TO BE BOILED, EVEN IF NOT COOKING THIS MUCH FOOD.

4 in.

4 in.

PLASTIC BAG TIED SHUT AROUND POT, TO KEEP HOT WATER VAPOR FROM DAMPENING INSULATION. A BAG IS DESIRABLE BUT NOT ESSENTIAL. TO PREVENT THE HOT POT FROM BREAKING THE BAG, FIRST COVER POT WITH TWO THICKNESSES OF NEWSPAPER.

4-in. OF INSULATION--NEWSPAPERS, CLOTH, ETC

LIDDED POT, PREFERABLY AT LEAST 9-in. IN DIAMETER.

Saving cooking fuel and work by making and using an "insulated nest."

—Many people have used a thermos bottle to finish cooking rice, wheat, beans, lentils and such. To cook brown rice, use 1⅓ cups brown rice, 2½ cups water, ½ tsp. salt and 1 tsp. salad oil. Bring to a boil and pour into a previously-heated thermos. Lay it on its side for 6 to 8 hours.

—Cook in a *bottle* if you do not have enough good pans. Fill one or more bottles with quick cooking vegetables. Cover

---

1. Civil Defense Research Project, Kearny, C. H.; Oak Ridge National Laboratory.

them with boiling water (to be used later). Screw on the lid and submerge in any old pan, bucket or kettle full of water. Cover the kettle and boil about 30 minutes.
—Line old baking pans with leaves before pouring in the batter for cakes and fruit bars. Use geranium leaves. (Use mint or nasturtium leaves when making meat loaves.)

Most people are not in the habit of cooking beans very often. (It is easier to open a can.) After experimenting a little and determining which pans to use and the length of cooking time, it will be easier to use them more often in our daily meals.

Cooking time varies with the type, age of the beans, and the hardness of water. Beans that have been sprouted will cook in about 30 minutes. If salt, tomatoes, catsup or vinegar are used in bean recipes, it will take longer for the beans to soften. Wait and add them after the beans are tender.

General directions for cooking pinto, kidney, navy and lima beans, whole dry peas and garbanzos:
—Soak 1 cup beans, etc. in 3 cups water for about six hours.
—Cook in the same water to retain flavor and nutrients for about 1½ hours. Yield about 2½ cups. To shorten soaking time, cover beans with cold water and boil for 2 minutes. Remove from the heat, leave lid on, soak for one hour, and then cook for the required time.

Wheat, rice, lentils and millet, for example, need no soaking. Add about two parts water to one part food and cook from 30 minutes to one hour. (For a soft millet, I cook one cup millet in four cups milk for one hour. Yield four cups.)

The live steam method of cooking is my preference for all grains, beans and legumes. (See *Passport to Survival,* page 29.) Try cooking wheat for about eight hours at 150° in a heat-controlled electric skillet using a rack, inset pan and dome lid.

Cooking Soybeans and Other Protein Foods

Careful home cooking and commercial processing techniques are required to preserve maximum protein quality. The protein in legumes is rendered more digestible by cooking, but high heating of cereals and milk causes adverse structural changes in the protein.[1]

_____

1. "Nutrition and Physical Fitness," page 92.

Maximum nutritive value of soybean protein is achieved by treatment with live steam for about 30 minutes[1] or by autoclaving at 15 pounds pressure for 15-20 minutes. This laboratory testing was done with ground whole soybeans. Overcooking of soybeans generally results in a bitter flavor. The reason heat improves the nutritive value of soybean protein appears to be related to the destruction of trypsin inhibitors that interfere with digestion.

For softer soybeans try this: Boil 1 cup beans in 3 cups water for 2 minutes. Cool and place in the freezing compartment of your refrigerator overnight in a flat pan. Crack to remove from the pan and cook as usual.

Food Preparation Suggestions
when Appliances are not Working

Invest in a good ball bearing rotary egg beater (if electric beaters are not operating), stainless steel strainers, graters, flour sifters, narrow bread pans, muffin tins, cookie sheets, sturdy bread boards (or better still, a chopping block), canners, colander and other non-electric food equipment.

Soybean Milk Without a Blender

a. Soak, cook and grind 2½ cups of soybeans.
b. Put the ground beans in a strong nylon bag.
c. Place the bean bag in a large flat pan.
d. Pour a gallon of hot water over the bag, a quart or two at a time.
e. Knead and press out the milk, and pour off into another container. The milk can be boiled or heated in a double boiler to take away the soybean taste.

Making juice without a juicer (for a person that cannot chew). Place a double thickness of nylon net, about 18 inches square, over a wide bowl. Stand a stainless steel grater on the net and grate vegetables or fruits. Remove grater. Bring ends of the net together, twist and press the juice into the bowl. Drink at once.

---

1. The charts in Smith and Circle's book, page 232, show very little change in the protein when cooking the beans an hour instead of 30 minutes. (Smith, Allan K., Ph.D., and Circle, Sidney J., Ph.D., "Soybean Chemistry and Technology," Vol. 1, The AUI Publishing Co., Inc., Box 81, Westport, Connecticut 06880, 1972.)

Mortar and Pestle — Seems every home should have one even if it is just a heavy door knob in a wooden bowl. How else would I grind a few spices, nuts or grains if my electric seed grinder did not work?

Grinding the grain (See Power and Fuel Shortages, p. 47)

Keeping Fresh Protein Foods and Vegetables [1]
Without Refrigeration

The shad fish we packed in salt two years ago is still good. The fish were cleaned, boned, and packed alternately with coarse rock salt in a plastic bucket. We started with a ½-inch layer of salt in the bucket and placed the fish, skin side down, in layers with ½-inch of salt over each layer. The top fish are skin side up, and a plate is laid over the top. After three days, pour off the water that has been drawn out of the fish. Cover and keep in a cool place. It is safe to eat this brined fish uncooked. Cut in small pieces and soak in several waters to get rid of the salt. Use in creamed dishes or salads in place of tuna fish.

Salting and brining of vegetables and fish.

1. See "Salting and Brining of Vegetables," page 100 "Passport to Survival."

Fish, poultry and meat will keep without spoiling at room temperature if treated with a POCO mix. This mix is a commercial product[1] made from wheat, corn and soybean meal which has been chilled and exposed to hickory smoke. This natural preservative and sea salt is rubbed into the item on both sides. After it hangs and dries for two or three days, it is kept in a dry place so it will not absorb moisture. In a month or two, it is ready to eat. Leave some of the mixture on and add a little oil to absorb the nutritious preservative.

Canning Tips[2]

Two recent books give over 350 pages of complete directions for preserving food: *Putting Food By* and *Stocking Up*.

Not many of us in the past have canned or bottled such things as soup, stew, meat, fish, sandwich spreads or nuts. In the future, I foresee many families preserving their food with whatever equipment they have.

One mother I know cans fish in a pressure cooker on a camp stove by a stream as fast as her husband catches the fish. Another lady filled quart jars with dry nuts, sealed with new lids and processed in 250° oven for 45 minutes. These were still fresh tasting after eight years.

A family fed their rabbits gallons of wormy raisins they had dried and left in a warm garage overnight for moths to lay eggs on. To prevent this loss, pack the raisins loosely in clean jars, place without lids in a 150° oven for 20 minutes and then cap with sealing lids. Or use a pressure cooker—five pounds for five minutes.

Gluten can be frozen, dried or bottled. (See pages 119 and 132 in *The Gluten Book*.)

Comfrey, dandelion greens or other "free greens" could be lightly steamed first, packed in sterile jars, then processed in a water bath for 30 minutes.

To keep fruit from darkening at the top of the jar, use ½ tsp. ascorbic acid powder to a quart jar, or a 250 mg. Vitamin C tablet.

Fruit canned without sugar or honey will keep as well as sweetened fruit, according to Kerr Glass Manufacturing Co.

---

1. Dr. J. D. Walters, M.D., has had several fish, for more than three years, preserved this way, and they have retained their original shape, color, texture and appearance. POCO mix is available from Sunshine Valley Foods, 8725 Remmet Avenue, Canoga Park, California 91304.

2. See Chapter 9 in "Passport to Survival" on "Food Preservation."

Chapter 16

Don't Let It Spoil

Fumigants

TODAY MORE AND MORE FAMILIES ARE STORING GRAINS. For those who want to treat their grains against weevil and other insects, consider the use of Perma-Guard D-10.[1] It is composed of a specifically stipulated diatomaceous earth and sold as a grain or seed storage insecticide for wheat, barley, buckwheat, oats, rye and to a lesser degree for corn, millet and rice. The milling, baking, nutritive and germination qualities of grain or seed are not affected when treated with this product. It feels like fine flour and has a bland chalky taste. It suffocates and dehydrates the insects.

Directions for use: One cup Perma-Guard powder is required for every 25 pounds of grain to be treated. Fill the storage container with alternate layers of grain and powder beginning with a three inch layer of grain and ending with a sprinkle of the powder. Seal and then shake or roll the container on its side to mix thoroughly. There is no need to remove the powder from food before milling or using any other way.

Diatomaceous earth is a fossil-type rock that was once single-celled water plants (diatoms) of different kinds. It contains trace minerals with silicon in greatest supply. This rock could cover a whole mountain top. One mine is in Steam Boat, Nevada. It is sold under many names and combined with other products to prevent mildew, rust, fungus and reduce moisture in foods. (It is even used in some lipsticks.) It is a valuable storage product

1. "Acres U.S.A.," April 1975, after months of research, recommends Perma-Guard for storage grains and seeds.

used as an insecticide for food and growing plants and to reduce moisture. It can be stored in a refined or crude state (that the Creator intended for our use).

Carbon Dioxide (CO_2) is safe and legal to use on grains and dried foods. It comes in two forms: cake (dry ice) or as a gas in a metal cylinder.

Procedure for using dry ice in cake form:

—Place a layer of grain (or other food) an inch deep on the bottom of a five gallon can or plastic bucket.

—Put two cubic inches of dry ice on a piece of folded newspaper. Blow off the frost. Crush to about 1/8 inch pieces with light blows from a hammer.

—Spread the crushed ice over the layer of wheat; immediately finish filling the can.

—Put the lid over the opening, but do not seal it tight for abut 30 minutes. (Otherwise, the can may bulge from gas produced as the dry ice evaporates and may blow the lid to the ceiling.) If a container should bulge, cautiously remove the lid for about two minutes and then replace it.

Some Fumigants are Illegal to Use

Many other products that have been used to successfully treat grains are now illegal to sell for use by homeowners. For example:

—Carbon tetrachloride and pure (USP) ethlene dichloride.

—Rock or lump sulfur—One ounce was put in a small perforated box inside a five gallon container of grain. Now, at least in the state of California, N.F. grade "Flowers of Sulfur" (which contains less arsenic than the crude lump sulfur) is the only grade that can be sold if it comes in contact with food stuffs. This is more odorous than crude sulfur.

Keeping Grains and Other Foods Cool and Dry

Freezing and Oven Method

Keep the temperature of the grain below 40°. Freezing the grain inactivates the weevil, but does not kill it. It may not be necessary to treat wheat at all if you are buying low moisture wheat (below 9 or 10 percent), and it is clean and stored in clean containers with tight lids. However, humid warm climates are an insect's paradise. In the Hawaiian Islands, for example, I shudder to think of the time I put my ear up to a barrel of untreated wheat and listened to the hum of weevil. In other areas, where the weather is warm and moist and where you are storing a small quantity of food at a time, reducing its moisture content is a good plan.

Oven Method — Place not more than ¾ inches wheat in a shallow pan and put the pan in a 150° oven for one or two hours (depending on how damp it is). Leave the door open slightly.

Calcium Chloride

To reduce the moisture in food, use the oven, sun, dehydrators or commercial products such as Silica-Gel, Absorb-All or calcium chloride. It is not sold for that purpose, yet it is a safe inexpensive product that draws moisture out of the air (or food). How to use calcium chloride:[1]

— Use two plastic containers that fit inside of each other. The top one is perforated and holds about 4 ounces of calcium chloride (for a five gallon can of grain).
— As it draws moisture, the liquid drips down into the bottom container. (A net bag and a bowl could be used instead.)
— Seal the container; inspect it occasionally and empty any moisture that has collected. Replace wet calcium chloride with dry.

Food Storage Containers

Food storage containers are getting more expensive, and it is worth the time and effort to take care of the ones we have.

Metal Containers—protecting from rust—sealing and storing
— Remove any rusty spots with steel wool. Wipe with a rag dipped in alcohol and dry with a clean cloth; then paint with Dry Swift Enamel or any rust deterrent.
— If paint is not available, any oil or grease rubbed on the can will help prevent rust, or coat it with a thin layer of paraffin wax.

---

1. Calcium chloride is cheaper in large cities where much concrete is used. It is an additive to concrete to help it set up faster and keep cement from freezing. It is also used on icy roads. Mason Supply Inc., at 2637 SE 12, Portland, Oregon 97242, sells an 80 pound bag for $10.66. (Price will increase.)

—Metal containers should not be allowed to touch cement walls or floors, as they will absorb moisture from the concrete, thus causing rust. Use slats, blocks, cardboard or rolled newspaper.

—The gold lining of some cans flakes off into the grain. To prevent this, put food in a plastic bag before placing in the can.

—Round tin cans with slip-over lids (using masking tape around the edge) are not air tight and grain that has been fumigated with a gas sometimes gets weevil in it. Why? In a warm, damp place, the gas could escape in time and the small larvae already in the wheat could emerge and live. Solution: Try using water-glass sold at a drug store around the seal.

Plastic Containers — Food in white rust-proof containers appeals to me. A good high density polyethylene food container should not shrink or crack. True, rats can chew through plastic buckets; so store rat traps (as well as mouse traps).

Contamination and Spoilage

To kill insects infesting dried fruit, drop the fruit in boiling water for about one minute. Spread the fruit to dry before storing.

Cockroaches and Pantry Pests — Boric acid kills cockroaches. Put no more than ½ tsp. in one place. Deposit in dark narrow inaccessible areas that roaches use for hiding.

Mold — Develops where it is dark and humid; light inhibits mold. A large amount of fresh wheat sprouts molded within a day or so in a plastic bag in the refrigerator.

Rancidity — Foods such as cornmeal, rice polish, whole wheat flour and other grains and legumes go rancid faster when ground. I have heard that some rancid foods can be detected by a burning in the mouth and throat. Rancid foods are destructive to some vitamins and cause other damage which is reason enough to guard against their use.

—Sunflower seeds, pumpkin seeds, pecans, shredded coconut or any food containing oils (and of course bottled or canned free flowing oils) go rancid in the presence of warmth and air. Rancid food is very detrimental to our health. The hydrogenated cooking fats in a can never go rancid, but digestive juices have a harder time breaking them down.

Spices used in cooking may retard rancidity — Caraway, cumin, fennel, cinnamon, cloves, pepper, tumeric and chilies used in India in curries and other food, are said to keep fats in food from going rancid.[1]

Old and New Ways of Keeping and Ripening Food

Wheat and grain are good insulators — Old timers put cured hams in the grain bins to keep them from the air and to keep cool.

Food in partially-filled containers keeps longer if transferred to smaller containers with little or no air space.

Unusual ways to increase the keeping qualities of food[2]— Reports are that wheat grass suspended above milk or meat (in a closed jar) will help keep them fresh. Tomato juice keeps better if stinging nettle has been planted around the tomato vines. Mold and putrefaction are retarded.

Ethylene gas given off by raw sliced apple will ripen other fruit such as avocado, pears, bananas in a covered pan. Lift the lid occasionally to let in the air.

Keeping Foods Cool

If our refrigerators are not running, how are we going to keep food cool? We can take advantage of the cold air from under the house. Old timers used to have open vents cut in the pantry floor underneath a screened food cupboard. Air blew up through the floor and kept things cool.

A friend tells of the "spring house" at her grandmother's—a small shed built over the running stream with crocks of food lowered in the water to keep cool.

Insulated carrying boxes may prevent food spoilage when going on a picnic or being at home without electricity. Inbetween temperatures of food, from very hot to very cold, are ideal for reproduction of the organisms that cause food poisoning. Styrofoam boxes are efficient but may not be available. If you have a sturdy cardboard box, newspaper, masking tape and aluminum foil, you may make a box that will keep hot foods hot and cold food cold for at least two hours.

Use a box with a lid that fits over the top. Insulate the lid with a one inch pad of newspaper covered with aluminum foil (shiny

---

1. "The Herbalist," page 187.
2. Hippocrates Health Institute, Boston.

side out). Fasten with masking tape. Keep the padding one inch from the edge of the box. Pad the sides and bottom of the box the same way.

Keeping Qualities of Food

Wheat lasts indefinitely if properly treated. However, some claim the oils in the wheat deteriorate significantly after 10 to 50 years. Other foods deteriorate at a more rapid rate:

Dry skim milk powder[1] (non-instant) — Seven years and longer.

Raw peanuts — Keep well for seven to eight years. Peanut butter, approximately four years.

Soybeans — Do not sprout well after two years. Some other beans sprout after five years.

Brown rice — starts to go rancid in two years.

Honey — Comb honey my father had for 40 years still tastes good. Ripe honey without added moisture keeps indefinitely.

Molasses — Good for four to five years.

Note: Storage conditions vary in every climate and every home, and the quality of food affects its longevity.

---

1. Dry milk that is hardened is still usable (if fresh tasting). Hit it with a hammer or a rolling pin to reduce it to a powder again.

Chapter 17

Special Section

Some Prepare—Some Don't

SOME PEOPLE BELIEVE this is the "11th hour" in preparing for a food shortage. They are making quick decisions on what to store. Others are reluctant to prepare, even though they know the hazards of weather, the threat of an oil shortage for farm machinery, and problems of distribution are real.

The Van Soost family from Holland, now living in Canada, are motivated to store food. During the war they lived through eight months of complete absence of foods in any stores. People paid as much as $30 (in today's American money) for a loaf of bread on the black market, and bartered their radios, wedding rings, linen, clothing and jewelry for food. It is difficult for those who have never experienced a food shortage to believe there could be one in this country.

Meals Away from Home

It may prove a blessing to have food on our shelves and in suitcases that we can grab quickly in case of earthquake, flood or other calamity. Perhaps a food supply is needed as we leave the cities on a trek into the back country off the main highways.

Hopefully, it is just food we will be needing for a school lunch, a shopping trip, a day at the zoo, backpacking, a package to a college student, or for a trip to a foreign land.

My daughter and I filled a travel bag with 30 pounds of food before leaving on a six-week trip to Europe. We had a U-Rail pass and were eating on the train much of the time. The dried fruit and nut bars individually wrapped were soon gone, and also the jerky, almonds and pumpkin seeds. Along the way we bought cheese and bread and never tired of alfalfa sprouts and buckwheat lettuce on our sandwiches. I enjoyed sprouting the seeds in plastic containers, growing the greens in small boxes of soil, and putting them in the sunny train window to turn green as we traveled along. Our seven-grain cereal mix, sprouted or just soaked overnight, was concealed in big soft figs that we ate while sightseeing. Homemade vegetable powder or a carob mixture added to hot water was a good beverage late at night. As a precaution against getting sick, we took 3,000 mg. of Vitamin C a day, 6 calcium tablets, 1 Vitamin E 400IU and two multivitamins. It was an interesting experiment. We stayed well and saved money, spending only about $75 for food during the six weeks in Europe.

In the future I may not always have jerky, pumpkin seeds or figs, but I intend to have:

—Five gallons of thin dry sliced bread.
—A quantity of dried fruit leather or blocks of dried ground fruit to slice and mix with nuts and seeds.
—Sunflower seeds (a big supply), wheat, rice, and corn for a parched seed mix.
—Vegetable broth.
—Commercial freeze-dried food.

A large family I know traveled in a van through Mexico. They took cases of home canned meat and vegetables. Stalks of bananas and other fruit were purchased there. Another friend sprouts wheat while traveling and eats a small amount every day, along with regular meals.

It seems that wherever we are on the face of the globe, under various circumstances, each individual can to a degree select the foods he needs to keep well. As we store food in our homes and return to the custom of more home prepared foods, we will have things on hand to take with us at a moment's notice should the need arise.

A new book, *Roughing It Easy*, has a chapter on camp meals and menus, with helpful shopping guides and planning all done for you. *Recipes for a Small Planet* has a chapter on how to eat balanced meals while camping.

Company Meals

Many times when I have company for a week and we are not home for every meal, before we leave the door, I grab a basket and fill it with food. One guest recently said, "Esther is the only person I know that can serve gourmet meals out of a basket."

When I know company is coming, I seldom shop at the supermarket. I prepare meals with the food I have. It does take some advanced planning, especially without using much meat. Before my guests arrive, I work fast to prepare:

—Soup stock, meatless loaves, patties, gluten or chili.
—Bread, rolls, bread sticks, corn bread and granola.
—Soy cheese (tofu).
—Ice cream using fresh or frozen fruit.
—Carrot juice, soaked prunes, boiled eggs.
—Pickled beets, onion and cabbage relish.

With tossed salads, fish and hopefully corn and tomatoes from the garden, what am I worried about? Nothing except the time it takes to prepare it. Maybe I will break away from tables laden with many foods, and just serve my guests soup and dried bread in the winter.

Changing Our Food Habits

Learning to like unfamiliar foods — Fathers, mothers, teenagers and toddlers do not always accept foods with the same enthusiasm at the same time. Most parents want first class food for the family like first class homes, schooling, clothes, music and literature. Some first class foods may be unfamiliar to some family members. Foods such as:

—All grains—including millet, barley and rye.
—Meatless loaves and patties, gluten and tofu.
—Strange greens in the salad.
—Green drinks, herb teas.
—Dried fruits and vegetables.

To foster acceptance of an unfamiliar food, try this: Rehearse in your mind about 25 times the food in connection with a very pleasant experience. If our brain receives an order, it will carry it out. Since it doesn't know the difference between what is actual physically experienced and what is vividly imagined, we can program our mind to accept and enjoy unfamiliar foods.

Food is a Family Affair

I knew a family where everyone helped prepare the food and a pact took place, "I'll eat what you fix, if you'll eat what I fix."

I do not think there is a boy or girl who succeeds in making beautiful whole wheat bread, or that takes their turn growing fresh alfalfa sprouts, that would refuse them at the table.

Getting children to eat what their parents eat usually is not hard to do. A new food could be served to Mom and Dad without offering any to the children until they ask, and then only a bite at a time. It is a privilege for them to be allowed to eat this special food. Adults who "like everything" usually were exposed to a great variety of foods in their younger years when they were more willing to try things.

Four of my grandchildren have learned to take at least one bite of anything that is served (like their daddy was taught to do). This policy strictly enforced has helped them enjoy a wide variety of food. Dr. Kurt W. Donsbach says: "A broad acceptance of food is an insurance policy against disease and is the groundwork for greater achievement in both mental and physical spheres of physical endeavor."[1]

—Eating falls within the realm of a child's responsibility.
—It is best for the child that mother not have strong feelings about food. She offers food of quality and taste, and trusts her children to eat as much as the appetite demands.
—Give a child a choice, such as a half glass of milk or a full one.
—Labeling certain foods as "health foods," doesn't always make them popular.
—Serve unfamiliar "survival" foods in gourmet style. Vary the shape and texture of food. Make the plate look as pretty as a picture. (I am surprised when I see mothers serve economy food in a sloppy, unprofessional, uncreative manner.)
—Arrange food on a child's plate in a scene—with moon and mountains, or as a flower, animal, object or person. (A face on anything is a delight to a child.)
—Out of sight, out of mind. Take away the foods you do not want eaten and replace with those you do.

Teen-age Conformity to Family Eating Patterns

Some teen-agers complain that their parents are too slow in changing over to more "natural foods." And other parents who

---

1. Dr. Kurt W. Donsbach, page 160-161.

have "made the change" are dismayed at the vocal lashing they have to contend with over the food in the house. Maybe some will listen to your reasoning that you want pretty daughters and strong sons—happy and intelligent. The whole reason parents work so hard for the family is to provide a first class environment for them, including the food they eat. This "punch line" is lost when they earn their own money and eat what and where they want.

I can give comfort to the parents of teen-agers (who do not always conform) from my own experience. When they marry and their health and wellbeing is their own responsibility, they will remember the example you set of good eating habits.

Eating Less

Some of our health problems are attributed to overeating. We can develop the habit of eating less at a meal.

I observed in several countries that much smaller amounts of food were served than Americans are used to. Two missionaries in Switzerland said for the first two months they were hungry all the time. After that, they were accustomed to smaller servings of food and never felt better in their lives.

Fewer refreshments can be served when food is scarce. In Holland one evening about 13 people were served a pound loaf of fruit cake cut in thin slices (one left over) and circled on a plate. Lemonade was served with it. On my return to the states, I was invited to join a discussion group in a home where the refreshments consisted of fresh fruit salad, ham, three kinds of cheese, potato chips and dip, cake and nut breads, punch, three kinds of candy and some nuts. It was good and I ate some of everything, but I was deep in thought over the contrast.

Approximately 19 percent of the United States national income is spent on food.[1] Of that 19 percent, 13 percent is spent on ice cream, coffee, candy, and soda pop! We consume 100 pounds more sugar per person annually now than we did in George Washington's time, when the average annual consumption was only 14 pounds per person.

It would help, I am sure, in learning to eat less, if we would survey our day's food supply. Put it all out on the cupboard, or list the available food for that day. Scarce food items could be

---

1. Deal, Dr. Sheldon C., "New Life Through Nutrition," New Life Publishing, 1001 North Swan Road, Tucson, Arizona 85711, pp. 7 & 156, 1974.

proportionately allotted to individual family members. (If you know you have eaten your portion, you are less likely to cheat and eat someone else's.)

A commercial food service company prepared daily food boxes for their customers. Precise amounts are weighed and packaged for each meal. This idea intended for weight reducing could be used occasionally at home.

Restraint in other people impresses me. A foreign student, living with us, had not eaten sweets for six years. I decided I could surely go for six months without sweets—and I did.

While visiting the Van Zoost family in Amsterdam for three days, not once did I see their children open the refrigerator or eat between meals. This was a shocking contrast to my own family's eating habits. And yet we weren't as permissive as a family I recall who had groceries delivered and the two children opened the lunch meat (and other things) and ate most of it before dinner.

Divert the Mind from Food

Behavior modification specialists tell us:

—Instead of turning to food for solace when we are unhappy, discouraged, worried, frightened, when we're feeling lonely, unloved or depressed, turn to other activities that give us pleasure: read, write, sing, call a friend, paint, knit, drink water or herb tea, walk, massage hands or feet, listen to educational tapes or music. Intrench in the mind a dozen things we can enjoy doing instead of eating. If our goal is to lose weight, our subconscious mind must be convinced of this, as well as the conscious mind.

The food on our table can become secondary to the topic of conversation. Benjamin Franklin's father was very wise:

...At the table he liked to have, as often as he could, some sensible friend or neighbor to converse with, and always took care to start some ingenious or useful topic for discourse, which might tend to improve the minds of his children. By this means, he turned our attention to what was good, just, and prudent in the conduct of life; and little or no notice was ever taken of what related to the victuals on the table....[1]

If food is scarce, or the variety monotonous, this suggestion is a good one.

1. "Autobiography of Benjamin Franklin," Books, Inc., New York, page 59.

Fasting

A recent television program on world food shortages suggested we get used to going without a meal now and again. This would not be hard for any of us; but I think most people, who for some unforseen reason had to go without food for a few days without ever having done so before, would be in a very negative frame of mind, and fear for life itself would have a paralyzing, destructive effect on all the body functions.

I have gone three days without food with no ill effects. A friend had been on a 12-day fast (drinking water only). On the 12th day he knocked at my door looking happy and healthy. I was surprised to find he had just been on a five-mile hike with his boys. I was most interested in the diary he kept of the reactions that his body and mind went through during a previous 21-day fast. He had a qualified practitioner carefully prepare him and guide him through his first fasting experiences.

I think fasting on occasion and denying yourself certain foods is an experience that may help us eat less and adjust to various situations more easily.

Healthy Babies

The aim of this book is to help families prepare *now* for emergencies. Having healthy children in mind and body would certainly make things easier on parents in times of stress.

It is rather overwhelming to know that the health of the baby begins before it is born. Imagine the Utopia if newlyweds cared enough about the health of their unborn child to be in top physical condition before and after they were married, so when conception took place, they could provide a superb physical inheritance for their child.

Advantages of Breast-feeding

—Think of the advantage of breast-feeding in an emergency situation, if there were no heat or lights or if the family had to leave home.
—Breast-fed babies are less susceptible to infectious conditions. The baby starts to manufacture his own antibodies when about six months old.
—Human milk normally has about five times more Vitamin C than cow's milk.

—Breast milk favors the development of desirable strains of bacteria in the intestinal tract of the newborn.

—Statistics show that women who nurse their babies are far less likely to get breast cancer.[1]

Human milk could alleviate the world shortage of food. California Public Health specialist, Dr. Derrick Jelliffe, says much starvation can be traced to the decline of breast-feeding and the increasing reliance on bottle feeding of products that are in short supply worldwide.[2]

Increased Milk Supply in Nursing Mothers

LaLeche League and other sources have much to say about increasing the mother's milk supply. Two of my daughters claim their milk supply increases when their bread intake is reduced to a minimum. They eat a variety of food in season (home grown when possible)—legumes, seeds, nuts, eggs, milk, meat sparingly, fresh vegetables, fruit juice and natural sweets, which contribute to healthy babies as well as adults.

Basic Guidelines for Baby Feeding

What should baby eat? — After weaning—if the usual fresh milk, meat, eggs, bananas, oranges and boxed baby cereal became unavailable in an emergency—what would we feed the baby? Could the baby eat the whole grains, beans, sprouts, seeds, nuts and raw vegetables eaten by the family?

I asked a pediatrician in Salt Lake City these and other questions related to conventional baby foods. He said, "Any nutritious food eaten by the family can be eaten by the child in a form suitable to his age and ability to chew, and of course starting out with small amounts."

A year-old child will show no dislike for the color of a "green drink" for example. (None of my 13 grandchildren refused it when they were babies.)

Snack foods are an important part of the total food intake and should be first class foods, not just sweet treats.

Child's taste buds — It is interesting that infants have 9,000 tongue spores (taste buds) and adults have only 3,000. This is significant for several reasons:

----

1. "Better Food for Better Babies," Larson, page 11.
2. Excerpt from "Paul Harvey News," July 11, 1974.

—Adult foods are often seasoned to stimulate our fading taste buds.

—Seemingly bland foods are tasty to a small child with extremely sensitive taste buds.

—Infants and children are more discriminating than adults in detecting slight differences in flavor. Sweet, sour, bitter and salty tastes to adults will be more so to a child. Concentrated foods like dried prune puree could be diluted for a more mild flavor.

Introducing New Foods

—The best time to introduce new foods is before they start walking. After that they are too busy to pay much attention to food.

—Give the baby a single taste of a new food. Serve it several times so he has more than one opportunity to try it.

—Never introduce a new food when the child is too tired to eat.

—Give small servings—about 1 Tbsp. for each year of the child's life—on play dinner-size plates. Giant servings give the older child a feeling of defeat before he begins a meal.

—Let the child feed himself as early as possible, even pouring his milk from a small pitcher. Put up with the mess.

—Last, but not least, remember to say a blessing on the baby's food.

"Starve that Baby" was the title of an article that suggested if we start very young to eat less, human beings would live longer and healthier by cutting their caloric intake ⅓ while continuing to maintain high vitamin, mineral and protein levels. Fat cells developed from improper baby foods remain throughout life.

Vitamin B promotes appetite — If a child is consistently a picky eater, maybe he is not getting all the Vitamin B he should. Remember, Vitamin B is water soluble and not very stable to heat. A minimum of processing and cooking will guard against Vitamin B shortages. Barley and rice cereal, high in Vitamin B, lightly cooked, are good for babies after they are weaned.

Birth of a Baby

Today most expectant mothers want to be in the best hospitals and under the care of the best doctors. Under normal situations this is advisable. However, there is a possibility that history will repeat itself as in *Gone With the Wind*—when doctors were too busy to bother about delivering babies.

Remember the scene when Melanie is about to have her baby. Scarlett O'Hara has run for the doctor. She cried, "Oh Doctor! You must come. Melanie is having her baby...the pains are getting hard, please doctor!"

"A baby? Great God," thundered the doctor.... "Are you crazy? I can't leave these men. They are dying—hundreds of them. I can't leave them for a damned baby. Get some woman to help you. Get my wife. Run along now. Don't bother me. There's nothing much to bringing a baby. Just tie up the cord...."

Tying the cord is the least problem in childbirth, it would seem, but in case you need to know how, here it is:

1. The cord is fat and blue when the baby is born. Wait until it is thin and white.

2. Use a sterile piece of cotton tape (a shoelace will do) 12 inches long and tie around the cord four inches from the baby's body.

3. Tie another knot two inches farther out. (Use square knots—bring left side of the tape over right side for first loop and right side over left side for second loop.) Tighten each loop as tied.

4. Cut the cord between the two knots with sterile scissors. A sterile dressing is put over the cut end of the cord and held in place with a band.[1]

I have no fear of childbirth, especially after my fifth baby was born at home unintentionally. All my brothers and sisters were born at home with the help of a midwife. In those days, one doctor served three counties and the nearest hospital was 60 miles away.

---

1. Two good books to read on this subject are "Emergency Childbirth" by George J. White, M.D., Police Training Foundation, 3412 Ruby Street, Franklin Park, Illinois, 60131 and "Childbirth Without Fear" by Grantly Dick-Read. This was my "Bible" 30 years ago. (Latest edition, 1972.)

Chapter 18

Observations of People, Plants and Living Things

I GRIEVED FOR FAMILIES in the heart of Hong Kong, London and Sidney, Australia, who did not have a shovel full of soil to turn over in the spring. To beautify, subdue and replenish the earth is part of our reason for being here.

A lady in an apartment in New York had a little potted violet as her only link with nature. I glanced at her one night as she sat quietly in a dimly lit room before retiring. She was holding her plant and examining the unfolding of the buds with a small flashlight. I felt her spirit of communion with a higher power.

And then there was a little boy who entered the kitchen, his arms loaded with fresh corn and tomatoes from the garden, and with a smile on his face said, "Mama, the world is getting better all the time."

I agree—seed time and harvest time make the world better for all of us. Growing things can be such a comfort. A mother of two sons who were killed in Vietnam said to me, "If it weren't for my roses looking at me through open windows and a garden to care for, I could never have survived the loneliness and heartache."

Howard Brooks, a pioneer in horticultural therapy, believes that gardening is preventive medicine and can be prescribed for anyone. "It relaxes and soothes you," he says, "while putting you in harmony with the earth, and it offers a way to remain productive."[1]

A young girl separated from her husband expressed similar feelings about an 18-inch strip of garden back of her apartment. Another lady told me after working with people in an office all day, the first thing she did at night was change her shoes and go to the garden.

1. "Modern Naturity Magazine," May 1977, page 6.

An experience I had in the Hawaiian Islands in December of 1963 taught me a priceless lesson in the life cycle of plants. Late one afternoon, while standing alone in a dense mango grove out in the country, I looked and listened. I was surrounded by a multitude of living things—not people, but birds singing, frogs leaping, vines creeping over tree stumps, gnats whirring over fallen fruit and fresh plants pushing vigorously through warm, moist earth.

I was subdued by the independence of nature in this isolated living community of plants, animals and insects—taking care of their own needs at an accelerated pace. I realized that in this tropical atmosphere (warm sun, wind and rain), conditions were ideal for vegetation to grow to maturity and return to the soil to replenish it as nature intended.

I felt I was an uninvited guest and that I should drop the fruit I had picked up and silently retrace my steps, leaving this paradise to those that belonged there. I felt a twinge of guilt at man's power to decrease these natural habitats and to do things his way, creating problems for all living things.

In the last several years, science has been proving that plants are intelligent beings—that is, they react to their emotional environment. They thrive or fail according to the vibrations they receive, and they even have a capacity to "remember" stimuli that produced a prior response in them.

What does all of this mean to you and to me as consumers, as gardeners, or simply as inhabitants of a world filled with growing things? It means that never again can we look upon vegetation with an unconcerned eye, for we share with everything a spiritual bond, born of an increasing awareness that we all are God's creatures.

Recently a man who owns a small plane said to me, "If I had to watch internal revolution and famine conditions, I would get in my plane and go up to a high altitude and point it straight down and just keep going." This remark was no doubt made in "jest," but it troubled me.

When trouble comes, we need to guard against such extreme reactions. We need to do some soul searching to understand the destiny of America, to be aware of God's plan for His people, to know the power of Satan and to appreciate our unique mission in life for the good of humanity.

Ezra Taft Benson gave a talk entitled "Do Not Despair." He gave 12 ways to defeat fear and depression: repentance, prayer, service, work, health, reading, blessings, periodic fasting, true friends, inspiring music, endurance and goals. He said, "A man who is pressing forward to accomplish worthy goals can soon put despondency under his feet." (He made reference to spiritual, mental, physical and social goals.)

A simple analogy has motivated me to prepare *now* for the future. In our previous home we had a long ravine on part of the property line. It was densely overgrown with wild blackberry vines. Our adventurous ten-year-old son used a machete knife and chopped a tunnel through the rank growth and briers to the light of day at the end of the 50 foot ravine. He was very persistent, hour after hour, day after day, sweat trickling over his dirty face, as he whacked to the right and left, overhead and under, to clear the way.

He was so excited after completing the job that he pleaded with me to please follow him through the tunnel. He had made it possible for me to get through, but I was far too busy with current demands in the house with younger children and duties. Besides, I envisioned getting jabbed with stiff branches and pricked with thorns, squatting and stooping to get through. It just seemed too difficult.

In jest I begged off. As the weeks went by, I began to feel guilty over not responding to his plea. One day, when it was convenient for me, I said, "Come on, son, I never did go through your tunnel; let's do it now." He was slow to respond, and then said in a downcast tone, "No, Mom, you can't get through. The vines have grown over and blocked the way."

Circumstances may prevent us from doing everything we think necessary to live an independent life. We will be blessed for doing what we can. Here is a brief summary:

1. Grow, use and store the best foods available.

2. Have equipment, fuel and know-how to cope with power and fuel shortages and natural disasters.

3. Have a "trial run" on the changed way of life to see how well prepared you are.

4. Take care of your health, relying less on drugs and medical care.

5. Store durable work shoes and fabrics. Learn to sew, repair shoes and make emergency footwear.

6. Be ready emotionally and spiritually for the days ahead.

So, dear friends, don't wait too long. Prepare now for the uphill climb into a brighter day!

Bibliography

SURVIVAL BOOKSHELF

Growing Your Own Food—Building the Soil

Rateaver, Bargyla and Gylver, *The Organic Method Primer*, published by the authors, 1973, Pauma Valley, California 92061.

Sunset, *Basic Gardening Illustrated*, 925 drawings and photographs, 1963, Lane Books, Menlo Park, California. By the editors of Sunset Books and Sunset Magazine.

Ridley, Clifford, *How to Grow Your Own Groceries for $100 a Year*, 1974, Hawkes Publishing Inc., 156 West 2170 South, Box 15711, Salt Lake City, Utah 84115.'.

Stout, Ruth and Richard Clemence, *The Ruth Stout No Work Garden Book*, 1971, Rodale Press, Inc., Emmaus, Pennsylvania 18049.

Tompkins, Peter and Christopher Bird, *The Secret Life of Plants,* 1972, Harper and Row, 10 East 53rd Street, New York, N.Y. 10022.

Rodale, J. I. and staff, *Encyclopedia of Organic Gardening - Complete Book of Composting - Organic Gardening and Farming Magazine.*

Acres, U.S.A., monthly paper published by Acres, U.S.A., 10227 East 61st Street, Raytown, Missouri 64133.

Natural Food and Farming Magazine, official journal of Natural Food Associates, P.O. Box 210, Atlanta, Texas 75551.

Bixby, E.H., *Your Friend and Mine*, 1970, Save Our Soil Books, P.O. Box 02012, Portland, Oregon 97202.

Hills, Lawrence D., *Comfrey Report*, 1974, Henry Doubleday Research Association, 20 Convent Lane, Bocking, Braintree, Essex, England.

Hills, Lawrence D., *Comfrey—Fodder, Food and Remedy,* 1976, Universe Books, 381 Park Avenue South, N.Y. 10016.

Mittleider, J. R., *More Food From Your Garden*, 1975, Woodbridge Press, P.O. Box 6189, Santa Barbara, California.

Food Chemistry and Nutrition, Diet and Health

Goodhart and Shilf, *Modern Nutrition in Health and Disease*, 1973, Lea Febiger Co., 600 S. Washington Square, Philadelphia, Pennsylvania 19106.

Gunthrie, Helen Andrews, *Introductory Nutrition*, 3rd edition, 1975, C. V. Mosby Co., 3301 Washington Blvd., St. Lewis, Missouri 63103.

Bogert, Briggs, Calloway, *Nutrition and Physical Fitness*, 9th edition, 1973, W.B. Saunders Company, West Washington Square, Philadelphia, Pennsylvania 19105.

Griffin, LaDean, *Is Any Sick Among You?*, 1974, Bi-World Publishers, P.O. Box 116, Provo, Utah 84601.

Yudkin, John, M.D., *Sweet and Dangerous*, 1972, Peter H. Wyden, Inc., 750 Third Avenue, New York, N.Y. 10017.

Deimel, Diana, *Vision Victory*, 1972, Chairu Publications, P.O. Box 744, Pasadena, California 91102.

Clark, Linda, *Get Well Naturally*, 1969, Arc Books, Inc., 219 Park Avenue South, New York, N.Y. 10003.

Donsbach, Kurt W., D.C., N.D., B.T.S., *Passport to Good Health*, 1972, Rayline Publishing Company, 1413 E. Edngr St., Santa Ana, California 92705.

Alsleben, Rudolph H., M.D. - Wilfrid E. Shute, M.D., *How to Survive the New Health Catastrophes*, 1973, Survival Publications, Inc., 710 North Euclid, Anaheim, California 92801.

Griffin, Edward G., *World Without Cancer*, 1974, American Media, P.O. Box 1365, Thousand Oaks, California 91360. (Two books, part I and II.)

Benner, Bircher, *Way to Positive Health, Nutrition Plan for Headache and Migraine - Nutrition Plan for Digestive Problems*. Other books on arthritis and rheumatism, etc., 1972, Nash Publishing Corp., 9255 Sunset Blvd., Los Angeles, California 90069.

Nutrition Today. The world's most widely read (22,970 people take this) nutrition journal. American Medical Association urges every doctor to subscribe to this scientific publication. (Made possible by the support of State of Florida, Dept. of Citrus, Campbell Soup Co., The Gerber products, and Kellogg Co.) Nutrition Today, Inc., 101 Ridgely Avenue, P.O. Box 465, Annapolis, Maryland 21404. Published bi-monthly — $12.50 for members of the Nutrition Today Society, $13.50 for other individuals. Other magazines—

Prevention — published by Rodale Press.

Let's Live — published by Oxford Industries, 444 N. Larchmont Boulevard, Los Angeles, California 90004.

Provoker — Written by John H. Tobe, St. Catharines, Ontario, Canada.

The Answer: Preventive Medicine, published monthly by H. Rudolph Alsleben, M.D., The Answer, 10632 Trask Avenue, Garden Grove, California 92643.

Cancer News Journal, published bi-monthly by the International Association of Cancer Victims and Friends, Inc., Box 707, Solana Beach, California 92075.

Towner, Bettie, 1978, *Cancer Holiday,* Greenlake Publishers, P.O. Box 25045, Northgate Station, Seattle, Washington 98125.

The Health Gazette, published by National Health Federation, Box 688, 211 W. Colorado Blvd., Monrovia, California 91016.

Charriere, Doris T., *Hidden Treasures of the Word of Wisdom,* 1978, Hawkes Publishing, Inc.

Meyer, Joseph E., *The Herbalist,* printed in the United States. Revised and enlarged edition, 1960. (No publisher's name given.)

Kirschner, H.E., M.D., *Nature's Healing Grasses,* 1960, H.C. White Publications, P.O. Box 8014, Riverside, California 92501.

Doctrine and Covenants, section 89. Revelation given through Joseph Smith the Prophet at Kirtland, Ohio, February 27, 1833, known as the Word of Wisdom.

You and Your Health. A new guide to family health in three volumes. For more information, write to You and Your Health, 1350 Villa Street, Mountain View, California 94042.

Franklin, Krauthamer, Tai, Tinchot, *The Heart Doctors' Heart Book*, 1974, Grosset and Dunlap, 51 Madison Avenue, New York, N.Y. 10010.

Wigmore, Ann, D.D., N.D. Ps.D., Ms.D., D.B.M., D.H.M., *Be Your Own Doctor,* 1964, Hemisphere Press, Inc., 263 Ninth Avenue, New York, (212) 243-8000, Health Digest #148, For Survival, Grow Organic Food Indoors! Other books and publications by Ann Wigmore and the staff at Hippocrates Health Institute, 25 Exeter Street, Boston, Massachusetts 02116.

Dikkers, Melchior Dr., *The Story of Trace Minerals,* 1972, Biological Science Publishing Co., 1111 Las Vegas, Blvd. South, Las Vegas, Nevada 89104.

Weir, Edith C., *Human Nutrition* (Report #2), Human Nutrition Research Division, Agricultural Research Service, United States Department of Agriculture, 1971.

Rodale, J.I. and staff, *Food and Nutrition - Prevention Method for Better Health - Encyclopedia of Common Diseases - Complete Book of Vitamins,* Rodale Books, Inc., Emmaus, Pennsylvania.

Smith, Allan K., Ph.D. and Sidney J. Circle, Ph.D., *Soybeans: Chemistry and Technology,* Volume 1, Proteins, 1972, The AVI Publishing Company, Inc., Box 831, Westport, Connecticut 06880.

Moulton, LeArta, *Nature's Medicine Chest*, 1974, 6 sets, 24 full color, 4 x 6 cards, photographs of nature's healing herbs with information of where to find the herb and instructions for use. New book to be released soon. Nature's Medicine Chest, Box 482, Provo, Utah 84601.

Deal, Dr. Sheldon C., *New Life Through Nutrition*, 1974, New Life Publishing Co., 1001 North Swan Road, Tucson, Arizona 85711.

Kadans, Joseph N.D., Ph.D., *Encyclopedia of Medicinal Herbs*, 1970, Arco Publishing Company, Inc., 219 Park Avenue South, New York, N.Y. 10008.

Family Preparedness, Storage, Preservation, Recipes

Dickey, Esther, *Passport to Survival*, 1969, Bookcraft, Inc., Box 268, Salt Lake City, Utah 84110. Also published by Random House, Inc., 201 East 50th Street, New York, N.Y. 10022.

Salsbury, Barbara, *Encyclopedia of Family Preparedness, Just in Case*, 1975, Bookcraft, Inc., Box 268, Salt Lake City, Utah 84110.

Ruff, Howard J., *Famine and Survival in America*, 1974, Publishers Press, Salt Lake City, Utah. (This should be cross indexed with Food Chemistry and Nutrition.)

Hertzberg, Ruth, Beatrice Vaughn, Janet Green, *Putting Food By*, 1973, The Stephen Greene Press, Brattleboro, Vermont 05301.

Stocking Up—How to Preserve the Foods You Grow Naturally, by the staff of Organic Gardening and Farming, 1973, Rodale Press, Emmaus, Pennsylvania 10849. Also *The Rodale Cookbook*.

Tyler, Lorraine Dilworth, *The Magic of Wheat Cookery*, 1974, Wheelwright Lithographing Edition, Magic Mill, Salt Lake City, Utah 84101.

Sudweeks, Deanna Smith and Suzanna Smith Welton, *Kitchen Magic*, 1974, Kitchen Magic, P.O. Box 558, Pleasant Grove, Utah 84062.

Laughlin, Ruth, *Natural Sweets and Treats*, 1973, Bookcraft, Inc., Box 268, Salt Lake City, Utah 84110.

Moulton, LeArta, *The Gluten Book*, 1974, The Gluten Co., Inc., P.O. Box 482, Provo, Utah 84601.

Lappe, Frances Moore, *Diet for a Small Planet*, 1971, Ballantine Books, Inc., 101 Fifth Avenue, New York, N.Y. 10003.

Ewald, Ellen Buchman, *Recipes for a Small Planet*, Ballantine Books, Inc., 101 Fifth Avenue, New York, N.Y. 10003.

Nelson, Louise E., *Project: Readiness*, 1974, Horizon Publishers & Distributors, 50 South 500 West, Bountiful, Utah 84010.

Hurd, Dr. Frank J., D.C. and Rosalie Hurd, B.S., *A Good Cook...Ten Talents*, 1968, Allegan Health Clinic, 120 Cutler Street, Allegan, Michigan 49010.

Emery, Carla, *Carla Emery's Old Fashioned Recipe Book*, 1977, Bantom Books, Inc., 666 Fifth Avenue, New York, New York 10019.

Reynolds, Bruford Scott, *How to Survive with Sprouting*, 1970, Hawkes Publishing, Inc., 156 West 2170 South, P.O. Box 15711, Salt Lake City, Utah 84115.

Hunter, Beatrice Trum, *The Natural Foods Cookbook*, 1967, Pyramid Publications, Inc., 444 Madison Avenue, New York, N.Y. 10022.

Hewitt, Jean, *The New York Times Natural Foods Cookbook*, 1971, Avon Books, a division of the Hearst Corporation, 959 Eighth Avenue, New York, N.Y. 10019.

Jones, Dorothea Van Gundy, *The Soybean Cookbook*, 1963, Arco Publishing Company, Inc., 219 Park Avenue South, New York, N.Y. 10003.

Wheeler, Emme, *Home Food Dehydration*, 1974, Craftsman and Met Press, Seattle, Washington.

Macmaniman, Gen, *Dry It, You'll Like It!* Living Food Dehydrators, P.O. Box 546, Fall City, Washington, 98024.

Thomas, Dian, *Roughing It Easy*, a unique ideabook for camping and cooking, 1974, Brigham Young University Press, Provo, Utah.

Gibbons, Euell, *Stalking the Wild Asparagus*, 1962, David McKay Company, Inc., 750 3rd Avenue, New York 10017.

Flack, Dora D., *Dry and Save*, 1976, Bookcraft, Inc., Salt Lake City, Utah.

Emergency Preparedness and Do It Yourself Books

London, L. H., *How to Beat the Gasoline and Power Shortage*, 1973, L. H. London Enterprises, P.O. Box 16297, Portland, Oregon 97216.

Halacy, D.S. Jr., *Solar Science Projects*, 1971, Scholastic Book Services, a division of Scholastic Magazines, Inc., 50 West 44th, New York City, New York.

Andersen, Arthur W., *Bee Prepared With Honey*, 1975, Horizon Publishers & Distributors, 50 South 500 West, Bountiful, Utah 84010.

Kearny, C. H., *How to Make and Use a Homemade, Large-Volume, Efficient Shelter-Ventilating Pump: The Kearny Air Pump*, 1972, Oak Ridge National Laboratory, Oak Ridge, Tennessee 37830. Operated by Union Carbide Corporation for the U.S. Atomic Energy Commission.

Kearny, C. H., *Trans-Pacific Fallout and Protective Countermeasures*, Oak Ridge National Laboratory, 1973.

Medical Self-Help Training: If Disaster Strikes and There is No Doctor, Public Health Service Publication No. 1042, U.S. Department of Defense, Office of Civil Defense.

Byrne, W. F. and M. C. Bell, *Livestock, Fallout and a Plan for Survival*, prepared for the Agricultural Extension Service, University of Tennessee, 1973, UT-AEC Agricultural Research Laboratory, Oak Ridge, Tennessee 37830.

Brace Research Institute, *How to Construct a Cheap Wind Machine for Pumping Water*, 1965; revised 1973, MacDonald College of McGill University, STE Anne De Belevue 800, Quebec, Canada.

Understanding Ourselves and Others

Covey, Stephen, *How to Succeed with People*, Deseret Book Company, Salt Lake City, Utah.

Harris, Thomas A., M.D., *I'm OK—You're OK*, 1967, Avon Books, a division of the Hearst Corporation, 959 Eighth Avenue, New York, New York 10019.

Andelin, Aubrey P., *Man of Steel and Velvet*, 1972, Bookcraft, Inc. (Pacific Press, Santa Barbara, P.O. Box 3738, Santa Barbara, California 93105.)

Andelin, Helen B., *Fascinating Womanhood*, Pacific Press, 1963.

Kimball, Spencer W., *The Miracle of Forgiveness*, 1969, Bookcraft, Inc., Box 268, Salt Lake City, Utah 84110. Also *Faith Precedes the Miracle*, 1972, Deseret Book Company, Salt Lake City, Utah.

Hotschnecker, M.D., Arnold A., *Will to Live*, 1951, T.Y. Crowell Publishers, 666 5th Avenue, New York, N.Y.

Rector, Hartman and Connie, *No More Strangers*, 3rd Volume, Bookcraft, Inc., Salt Lake City, Utah.

Showalter, Annette, *Awakening Learning Awareness Center*, Portland, Oregon.

Pendlebury, Jim, *Behavioral Genetics Profile*, Portland, Oregon.

Preserving Our Freedoms—Understanding Our World

Benson, Ezra Taft, *God, Family, Country, Our Three Loyalties*, 1974, Deseret Book Company, Salt Lake City, Utah. Also, *An Enemy Hath Done This*, 1969, Parliament Publishers, Inc., 1168 South Main Street, Salt Lake City, Utah.

Skousen, W. Cleon, *The Naked Capitalist,* a review and commentary on Dr. Carroll Quigley's book, *Tragedy and Hope, A History of the World in Our Time.* Published as a private edition by the Reviewer, 1970, 2197 Berkeley Street, Salt Lake City, Utah.

Andersen, H. Verlan, *The Great and Abominable Church of the Devil, a Satanic World-wide Organization Foretold.* Provo, Utah, 1972. Order from Americans for Constitutional Government, P.O. Box 321, Provo, Utah 84601.

Toffler, Alvin, *Future Shock,* 1970, Random House, Inc., 201 East 50th Street, New York, N.Y. 10019.

Preston, Robert L., *How to Prepare for the Coming Crash - Wake Up America - The Plot to Replace the Constitution,* 1971-1972, Hawkes Publications, 4663 Rainbow Drive, Salt Lake City, Utah 84107.

Smoot, Dan, *The Business End of Goverment—How Federal Regulators Threaten to Destroy the American Businessman,* 1973, Western Islands, Belmont, Massachusetts 02178.

The Freemen Digest, published monthly by the Freemen Institute, 1331 South State Street, P.O. Box G, Provo, Utah 84601.

The Constitution of the United States of America, recorded on cassette tapes with teaching manual and commentary. Flick-Reedy Corporation, 7N015 York Road, Bensenville, Illinois 60106.

The Utah Independent, Dedicated to the Constitution, Liberty, Morality, and Truth. A weekly paper. 57 East Oakland Avenue, Salt Lake City, Utah 84115.

Index